Tempus ORAL HISTORY *Series*

voices of
Kent and East Sussex
Hop Pickers

The author loading Boadicea hops for planting out. (Photo courtesy of Iain Ross-McLeod)

Tempus ORAL HISTORY *Series*

voices of
Kent and East Sussex
Hop Pickers

Hilary Heffernan

Frontispiece: *Happy to be hopping in 2004.*

First published 2004

Tempus Publishing Limited
The Mill, Brimscombe Port,
Stroud, Gloucestershire, GL5 2QG

British Library Cataloguing in Publication Data.
A catalogue record for this book is available from the British Library.

ISBN 0 7524 3240 0

Typesetting and origination by Tempus Publishing Limited
Printed in Great Britain

Contents

List of Contributors

My sincere thanks go to the following contributors who supplied many stories, photographs and information used in this book: without their support it would not have been written. My apologies to any contributor, person or company whose material I have included and inadvertently omitted to acknowledge. My particular thanks are due to John and Kitty Liddell for their consistent support and generous hospitality; the Kent and East Sussex Railway who allowed the use of their railway photographs, Sergeant Del Fairs and Co.; Iain Ross-MacLeod who accompanied me on my research forays and whose keenly observed photographs help to represent many aspects of the hop industry; Bob Dockerty of Larkins, Miles Jennings of Harvey's; Stephen Lehman and John and Peter Cyster of Rother Valley who all supplied photographs and the hospitality of their breweries.

If you have a hopping tale to share why not send it to me c/o Tempus Publishers?

Mary Abell, Nancy Arrowsmith, Kath Balkham, Patricia Bathurst, George Bennett, Ian Bennett, Pat Bevan, George D. Blackman, Terry Blackman, Freda Blois, Mrs M. Boneham, Patsy Burgess, Horace Arthur Carr, Ann Casson, Stephanie Cater, Henry Chambers, Jack Chambers, Pełar Chopolski, David Coleman, Adele Coles, Roy Coles, Patrick Connor, Ray Cooper, Bill Covil, Catherine Creed, Peter and John Cyster, Ivy Dixon, Mark Dobler, Bob Dockerty, Pat Etherington, Rose Ethrington, Reg Evans, Sidney Fagan, Jenny Farrant, Peggy Farrant, Ann and Brian Feist, Irene Feist, Harry Golding, Freddie Grammy, George Green, Rhoda and John Grimes, Pauline Hawker, Margaret and Brian Hemsley, Bill Hill, Mrs D. Isaacs , Ilyam Ivanov, Joseph James, Roger Jeffries, Miles Jenner, Ivy King, Ellen Lanksford, Tricia Latham, Stephen Leman, Joan Lewer, Ron Leonard, John and Kitty Liddell, George and Elsie Maddock, Roy Martin, Mary Matthews, Sharman Mayhew, Peter Maylem, Joan Medill, John Miller, Sally Nattcutt, Val Noakes, D. Palmer, Liz and Sylv Parkin, Jill Poile, F.W. Pooke, Kathy Powell, Fran Price, Maud Reynold, Alfred H. Robinson, Iain Ross-MacLeod, Maurice Sargent, Colin Smith, David Taylor, Peter Veness, Ivan Vlaev, Mr J. Waites, Tricia Walker, Pat Walkling, Marion and Bill Weeding, Bill Wheatley, Jean and Irene Wilkins, Ellen Wilson Joan and Babs Wood.

Extract from the *Kentish Express*, 3 October 1903:
Having been paid off from hop-picking, a labourer, of no fixed abode, named Henry Mac Donald, imbibed too freely of intoxicating liquors, and commenced to create a disturbance in the village of Molash. He was requested to be quiet by P.C. Harry Newman, but he refused, and continuing his riotous behaviour he was arrested. So great was his violence that the assistance of four men had to be obtained to hand-cuff him to take him to the Ashford police station. His Worship imposed the fine of 5s., with 13s costs, but having spent his hop-picking earnings the prisoner was compelled to accept the alternative of 14 days' hard labour.

Extract from the *Kentish Express*, 2 October 1953:
Although Ashford Divisional Executive is concerned about children still absent from school because of hop picking, they feel it is no use taking legal action. Parents spent holidays in hop gardens and had a legal right to take their children.

Introduction

As the year progressed towards August, letters from the Kent and Sussex countryside dropped through letter boxes across the two counties, and in the sooty streets of London, seasoned Hoppers were already planning how they would travel to their particular hop field. There were plenty of choices: get together with the neighbours and hire a lorry between five or six families, all travelling down together with their belongings; cadge a lift from a costermonger friend and share his cart; walk, if it was a mere ten miles or so; push the family hopping barrow across London and catch the 4.00 a.m. 'Hoppers' Special' milk train to Paddock Wood or the station nearest to their hop garden; or go into Maidstone and catch one of the buses specially laid on to take workers to the hop fields and maybe transfer your belongings to the Kent and East Sussex Railway at Robertsbridge or Tenterden for Bodiam, or one of the stations in between.

For many folk this was a way of life, their parents and several generations before them would have gone hopping on the same farm, keeping the same family-furnished hop hut for several generations. This was their annual holiday. They had worked hard for it. How could it possibly end?

An important point about hopping was that the money earned was seldom 'spare'. It was an essential part of the family budget without which there would be nothing to pay for new boots or shoes for fast growing children, no money to catch up on rent arrears and nothing to pay for a Christmas dinner or small presents for the children. The majority of people lived in rented accommodation at that time; wages were far too low to consider buying a house, even though in the 1930s it was possible to buy a three-bedroom house for £400.

Wartime was an era when a luxury Christmas feast was roast chicken, baked potatoes, sprouts and home-made stuffing. Fruity Christmas cakes were rare as dried fruit had to be imported and all imports were suspended during the war, and brandy or rum were on ration. Anything a working family's children received at Christmas was gladly received. Every child hung up one of dad's old socks hoping there was a Father Christmas that year. On Christmas morning they would find an orange or tangerine wrapped in silver paper, a shiny copper penny or silver sixpence, a penny whistle, a soft silvery ball on a piece of elastic, a pack of 'Snap' or 'Old Maid' cards and maybe some sweets. A second-hand book or teddy bear may be added if the hopping money stretched to it. If Dad or an older brother was adept with a penknife there may be a carved wooden boat or other toy peeping out of the top of the sock and Mum may have saved enough coupons to buy wool to knit a pullover or socks. Clothing was an accepted part of Christmas presents. Computers and Game Boys had not been invented and even if they had, the working population had no money or time to spare for such luxuries. Despite the simplicity of presents they were always kept as a surprise, eagerly opened on Christmas morning and proudly displayed to family and friends.

Lives were radically changed when mechanisation came on the scene in the late 1950s-1960s. The cost of a pint was gradually rising due to increased wages, a rise in fuel prices and the general cost of modernising the industry. In the 1950s a new machine was invented which was to revolutionize the hop-picking industry which, Hoppers learned to their alarm, could not only pick a hop garden clean in less time than it took a 1,000 workers, but which required only a handful of employees to do the same job. These first monstrous machines were used in Worcester, but by the end of the 1960s some larger farms in Kent and Sussex had installed them, doing away completely with the need to hire individual pickers to deal with the bines. The days of Londoners coming to Kent and Sussex for a working holiday were nearly over.

Hop production costs gradually rose over the years and foreign freeze-dried hop pellets were proving a cheaper option. The bulk of hops are grown to produce the mash needed as the basis for beer-making but the cream of hop varieties are those providing the subtle and unique flavours by which individual beers are known.

Each variety of hop releases its own individual bouquet, from the mellow strains of Kent and Sussex Goldings to the tangier Progress and Phoenix, but as imported hops became cheaper, the demand for home grown varieties declined. In the 1970s and '80s, acre upon acre of hop gardens fell fallow as brewery demands on local hop farmers lessened. The decline of Kent and Sussex hop gardens had begun and with it, the chance for hopping holidays and that essential extra cash for underprivileged Londoners.

A few farmers experimented with developing American hops, hoping these would be more resistant to blight and other diseases. Some of these American varieties were Cascade, Hallertauer, Cluster, Tettnanger and Saaz. In nearly all these cases farmers reverted to the well tried and tested Kent and East Sussex hops.

But it wasn't only Hoppers and farmers whose lives were changing due to the lower demand for English hops. Breweries too were experiencing difficulties. With local hops subject to the vagaries of British weather, mildew, blight and related problems and the rising costs of brewing as well as an influx of foreign beers and lagers, the importation of freeze-dried hops reduced outlay and avoided the disaster brought on by crop failures. For the most part, local brewers still prefer Kentish and local hops such as Goldings, Fuggles and Phoenix for subtleties of flavour, but the bulk of brewing hops began coming in from Europe and only a handful of privately run breweries now get theirs from local gardens.

Farmers traditionally relied on a second string to their farming bow in case hop crops failed; fruit orchards, vegetable crops, pig and dairy farming had all proved useful standbys in the past but progressively these became mainstays as breweries looked elsewhere for their staple hop supplies.

Despite these difficulties and the sharp decline in the demand for English hops, traditional brewing is still alive in Kent and Sussex. A wide variety of lip-smacking real English beers, ales and porter made from local hops is readily available from small breweries scattered across the counties. These were the beers enjoyed by Hoppers on warm evenings in the local villages after a day in the gardens picking hops; the end product of all that hard work.

Railways were hit financially by this decline as they were no longer required to cater for many thousands of Hoppers traversing the South East of England to the gardens and back. Smaller, formerly indispensable lines were forced to close after losing these seasonal travellers as local passengers provided insufficient funds to cover costs. One such line was the Kent and East Sussex Railway which at one time ran an essential relay for Hoppers arriving on trains from London Bridge stations to Tenterden down through Guinness hop farming country as far as Bodiam.

Hoppers have long memories, and tales are still told of hardship, adventures, mishaps, wartime misfortune and laughter all experienced during their hard-working annual holidays among the bines. Here are first hand reminiscences galore, not only from Kent but also from Sussex Hoppers, local brewers, farmers and the Kent and East Sussex Hoppers' railway. Nostalgia is a celebration of our past, so read on and enjoy these unique anecdotes from the folk who were there.

1 Hoppers' Tales

The daily grind and vicissitudes of hop picking are remembered with pride and near affection by many Hoppers. Some, of course, hated the work. This was mainly because of the sometimes overpowering smell of hops, brown-stained hands, scratches from bines and many hardships that went with the work, but people still went because it was one of the few ways they could earn extra money over whatever regular weekly wages the family members brought in. The spirit of Charles Dickens' Mr Micawber, capable of making the best of the direst situation, stood in good stead here. No matter what problems they faced, Hoppers met them all head on, made jokes and songs about them and carried on working, optimistic that things would eventually turn out in their favour despite wet weather or burning sun, ultra-early mornings with wet dew, muddy fields where many a welly got stuck in the mire. Meanwhile Luftwaffe pilots strafed the hop gardens, bombs fell, enemy and friendly aircraft crashed nearby as Hoppers worked, sore hands infected by bine scratches turned septic, allergy rashes, nauseating latrines deep in dark woods, long late night walks in the rain back to the huts with dinner still to cook on an open fire, lack of money, inadequate clothing; these were all part of a hop picker's annual holiday in the gardens of Kent and East Sussex. Set against these trials were the recompenses: the health benefits of breathing clean country air after living the major part of the year in city smog, time to sing together as they worked, the excitement of being in the countryside, fresh fruit and vegetables and a rabbit (or chicken!) caught by themselves, a chance to walk in the countryside savouring a different way of life to

Hop picking at Hastings. Back row: Jane Burton, Gordon Boxall, Esther Boxall, Julie Wilson, Daphne Wilson. Front row: Sarah Wilson, Jacqueline Wilson, Susan Burton.

their usual hard grind to make ends meet and pay the rent. It is all remembered with justifiable pride that, whatever the adversity, they were still able to cope and came out smiling and on top.

A hard-earned gift

We were a regular hop picking family and hopped down in Kent every season.

One year I decided to buy my mum something special and, after much thought, secretly settled on a set of pretty plates with flowers round the edges. They cost more than I could afford but I knew that if I was careful, worked hard and picked lots of hops there was a chance that I would be able to earn enough to cover it.

I picked with great determination all six weeks of the season and when I was handed my pay on the last day I couldn't wait to get up to the shop back home in London. What if they had all been sold? But no, there they were, still on display in the shop window and I proudly handed over my hard-earned cash in exchange for the plates, watching anxiously as the assistant carefully interleaved every one with newspaper so I could carry them home safely.

Mum was really stunned when I presented them to her. They were kept as her 'best' and when she was old she gave them back to me, still in good condition. I still have them as a happy reminder of my hopping days.

Henry Chambers

When we were novice Hoppers

What with Mum being a novice at hopping, she wasn't sure what to pack for us to take down with us, so all our blankets were tied up with string and our clothes were pushed into pillowcases. When the lorry came to take us down to the farm we all piled on the back with Pat's pram beside us, overflowing with goodness knows what. It was so exciting driving down there and we couldn't wait to arrive. Then we saw the old hut we had to sleep in. 'Where's the bed?' we wanted to know, not thinking that we would have to sleep on the floor on a bed we'd have to make ourselves of faggots (cut branches) topped with scratchy straw, and that we would all have to sleep together in a long line.

Sally Nattcutt

Rats on the run

I live in Spain now but well remember my Kent hop picking days as a child. We hated using the toilets which were chemical and smelly. One day when I was dying to go I waited while the other kids all went off to buy an ice cream from the 'stop me and buy one' man, then ran right down to the end of an empty drift and crouched down there behind some discarded bines. When I stood up my face got caught on one of the horizontal wires and it threw me backwards

unexpectedly. I landed awkwardly on the side of my knee which hit the top of a cut-off tree stump. It really hurt but I didn't say anything to my mum. That night, as I was lying on the palliasse in the big, communal bed trying to get some sleep and listening to the sounds of scuttling mice round the hut, I felt something bite me on the foot. I stood up in the middle of the bed and yelled 'There's a rat in the 'ut!' and everyone made to scramble out in a panic. In the rush I lost my balance, fell backwards and sat on my auntie's face! When they lit the paraffin lamp the grown-ups discovered I hadn't been bitten at all, never mind by a rat; it was my swollen knee causing pains to run down my leg into my foot and making it hurt. When daylight came they took me to the Hoppers' Hospital to have it seen to, and then it was back to the picking.

Anon. visitor to the Age Exchange Reminiscence Centre, Blackheath

Hopping through the holidays

Many Hoppers were costermongers. They used their working horses and carts to take hopping boxes and furniture down for their holiday and that included everything they needed; even Grandma's chair. When we were about to come back to London after a fortnight's picking the farmer always asked 'Are you and your family coming back next year?' and he'd put our family's name down on his list. It was marvellous for us kids in the school holidays. We really looked forward to it and it gave us something to do as we were expected to pick hops too. After we'd picked as much as mum told us, we were allowed to go off and have all the fun of the countryside such as exploring and jumping in the pond for a swim.

Freda Blois

Nanny Denham

My gran was a real character. She was all go. When the foreman called 'Pull no more bines!' she'd go off and pull an extra five or six so she could keep on picking after the others had finished and earn more money for it. What's more she put all the leaves in as well so it looked like there was more than there was. We picked at Paddock Wood and Goudhurst. We always went scrumping in the nearby orchards if no-one was looking. Grandfather was always on the look-out for a bit of extra cash and he'd go into pub bars and tell the customers stories in exchange for a few pennies. This was called 'monologuing'. When he got back home at night, Nanny Denham would wait until after he'd gone to bed and dropped asleep then take all the pennies out of his trouser pockets to add to the housekeeping money.

Roy Martin

Memories of picking at Bodiam

From the age of two years old we came hop picking with our mother. We lived in the Old Kent Road and we never got away on a real holiday. As soon as August came, usually towards the end of it, we couldn't wait for that little brown envelope to come through the door and were so excited to have four weeks off school. The weather was always sunny, like it is now, and we just loved everything about it: the picking of the hops, the cooking, and days out in the fresh air. Our mother used to make the most wonderful suet puddings with syrup and jam or spotted dick. She would wrap them in a piece of cheese cloth to boil over the fire and they were so tasty. We used to get up very early in the morning and we always helped my mother pick. She gave us little treats when the tally man came round; sometimes it would be an ice cream, a little cake or something like that. We often picked into an umbrella or a little drum and when it was full my mother used to say 'I'll give you "so much" for what you've picked'. Now my sister and I are seventy-two years old – or seventy-two years young, and hardly ever does a month go by without us visiting Bodiam because, for one thing, we've had a tree planted in the National Trust grounds of Bodiam Castle just across the fields from the hop garden for our mother, who absolutely loved Bodiam. It's a chestnut tree because we remember she was always singing 'Underneath the spreading chestnut tree…' and when my sister and I come here every time we sit and have our lunch under her tree. George Bailey, the one who looks after the castle grounds, has put a seat quite near the tree so we can sit and enjoy it.

Jean Wilkins

Autumn fruits

After we had finished hopping, of an evening it was very nice. We'd all sit round the camp fire and sing songs and drink lovely mugs of cocoa. At weekends we'd enjoy going blackberry picking, and our mother would make apple pies and such. They were really happy times.

Irene, Jean Wilkin's sister

A soldier of three wars

I used to come to Craneham Woods in Bodiam. I was here when war broke out in 1939. I was with my grandfather, nan, mother, aunt and brothers. My oldest brother was Bill and then there was Alfie. I can remember it all very well indeed; the memories stand out a mile. We used to have a pole puller called Charlie and he ran through the hop fields shouting out to everybody 'War's been declared! War's been declared!' so we knew what was on. But I had to laugh because my granddad turned round and said 'well we've got to finish the job first'. So we did, but what it was all about was he wanted to get back home to join up, because although he'd been in the Boer War, at least the end of it, plus the First World War he actually wanted to get into this war, which he did until they found his age out. But coming back to Bodiam, it's not altered much outside the castle, because The Castle, the actual pub, is still there where we used to get our subs from at the end of the week to keep us going.

Freddie Ganny

So many recollections

Some of the fields, particularly Ewham and Northiam, were quite a long walk from our huts. It got very dark in the evenings and was often really cold, so no-one was particularly keen to wander off in the evenings. When the fire was lit we couldn't see much beyond it as there was no lighting on either the roads or in the farm yard. We children slept seven in a bed, head to toe. If someone turned over it meant we all had to grab at the blanket, especially if you slept at the edge of the bed. If you were too slow you had to do without. We loved to cook potatoes in the embers of the fire. They got really black and burnt on the outside and when you'd finished eating it with a pinch of salt your face was all blackened with soot.

Terry Blackman

Swan song

My dad had a good voice and one year when he went down hopping I wrote out the words of 'Talk of the Town' for him to sing at one of the campfires we had after dinner in the evenings. When he dropped dead of that Thursday morning, he still had the song in his pocket. He did go out of the world bad, poor dad.

Anon. contributor visiting the Age Exchange, Blackheath

Back home in London

We wore black lace-up boots to school with Blakey's studs on the tips of the soles and heels to stop them wearing out so fast. They clicked with a really satisfying sound as we walked on the hard pavements. If someone was running down the street you could hear them coming a mile off. If there was snow with ice the studs were great on the slides we made on the pavements and you went like a rocket! Dad was a porter in Covent Garden. He was great at his job and could carry any number of boxes or baskets on his head. If it rained there was no work as it wasn't safe to carry the boxes balanced on a wet hat in the rain. Our gran lived with us and, with a big family and as money was short, her pension really helped out. We lived in Bermondsey, Southwark, so it wasn't too far for Dad to get to work in the early mornings.

Terry Blackman

The boxing brothers

Down at Craneham Woods Farm in Bodiam we had two brothers who went picking and were both boxers; Alf Danahard and his brother. One of them actually fought Eric Boon for the welter weight championship of Great Britain. The wonderful thing about this time was that we can always remember it as it was and in those days we had some marvellous times. I have been back to where we picked several times now and found certain areas which I've found out a lot about. I've also been to Horsemonden to Ben Wheeler's Farm in Kent and that was another wonderful experience of people I used to meet. The Star and Winch pub is still there, The Ball may have gone. We used to have people come round the hop fields selling what we called wet fish, and I can tell you what, it was absolutely gorgeous and we used to buy it if we could afford it. We'd have half each of cod, haddock or whatever was for sale. We also used to have Hotspur Cake. This was a cake like a sponge but it had a beautiful pink cream on the top and I used to love it. My other great delight when we were hop picking was getting the daily comics late in the day, which sometimes had songs printed in them and one of the finest songs we got that way was 'South of the Border, down Mexico way'. All the old songs like 'Knees up Mother Brown' and 'In my mother's eyes'. It was wonderful to sit round in the evenings – someone used to bring a piano accordion and we'd all sit round and sing. I know they were hard times but they were some of the happiest times of my life.

Freddie Ganny

A healthy life

In 1938 we moved from Bermondsey to a house in Downham because my sister had an enlarged heart and the fresh country air was better for her there. The house was lit by gaslight and the narrow gas pipe sticking out of the wall had an attachment for a silk gauze gas mantle like the kind you sometimes see in caravans where they use bottled gas for lighting. The mantles went hard after they had been alight and if you touched them even slightly a little hole appeared where the silk had crumbled. Hopping wasn't really a holiday for us because we needed the money to supply the necessities of life. Hop picking meant cash, which was why we were such dedicated, almost ferocious pickers. At weekends we could sub from the money we'd earned from a little man from the farm who looked like Uriah Heap and came round the fields with his accounts book so he knew how much we had earned and how much we could sub. Some Hoppers subbed all their money for drink and had nothing left by the time they went home to London.

Terry Blackman

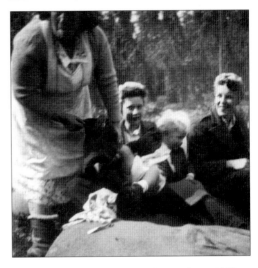

Vie Overall, Josie and Nell Booth at Bodiam, 1950s. (Courtesy Mrs D. Sargent)

Whatever's happened to little Tommy?

Our family hopped at Paddock Wood on the Whitbread farms. We had brick-built hop huts which were comfortable compared with some others we knew. We had double bunk beds and used striped ticking filled with straw for our mattresses. It was great for us kids because just before our August summer holidays ended our family set off to do three weeks' hop picking, so got extra holidays. I was only ten or eleven at the time. On the day we were due to go down we all met at my Nan's house which was at No. 102, Creek Road, Deptford. We travelled down on the back of an open-backed lorry with all our hopping boxes and things. When she climbed up onto the lorry we could see my Mum's long pink bloomers. Before we set off on the journey proper the adults called in at the Duke of Edinburgh pub for a drink and we kids were given crisps, arrowroot biscuits and orange juice.

Mrs Isaac's cousin Jabey and bushel basket with cousin Doris and family at Harts Green, 1920s.

Violet and Pat Cornwell from St Leonards on Sea down hopping at Newhouse Farm, Bodiam, September 1949. (Courtesy Mrs D. Sargent)

One year we got halfway down to the farm when my auntie said 'Where's Tommy?' He was our littlest. He wasn't on the lorry and we had to drive all the way back to the Duke of Edinburgh for him where he was still waiting outside the pub, sitting in his pushchair! Everyone sang from the back of the lorry all the way down to Paddock Wood.

Bill Wheatley

Life was not all hard work

If we got a sub at the weekends we'd walk along the lane and up the hill to Staplecross and catch the train down to Hastings. Sometimes Mum treated us to a bunch of grapes or we'd have an Italian ice cream – not like the stuff we buy today, but real ice cream made with thick cream and delicious to eat. If we had worked hard at the hops she took us all to the cinema to see a black and white film (there were few colour films then). Her favourites were Tyrone Power and Errol Flynn; real swashbuckling adventure films. We'd come back home afterwards and have sword fights in the garden, using long pieces of wood.

Terry Blackman

My queen of the hops

I know a place, never far from mind,
Where happy memories firmly bind
Me to my past;
A place to which I fondly flee
Whenever this world troubles me,
Where my thoughts are cast.
Down to the gardens and flourishing cones
Of hops where Mrs Roberts moans
Of measurer's tally,
I picture one with slim arms bare,
Singing as if she'd never a care;
My sweetheart, Sally.
I knew that she might laugh at me
As I got down on bended knee
Beneath the bine,
But Sally smiled and understood,
And then she sweetly said she would –
She would be mine.
We never rued that happy day
And were married on the fourth of May
At Five Oaks Green.
But that was three score years ago.
Now I miss my little helpmeet beau;
My hopping queen.

H.H.

'To earn a bob or two... '

Back in the 1950s when my mum and dad were struggling to bring up a family of six children, come September time we would all go 'Hopping' like hundreds of other families around our area. We originally used to catch the early morning farmer's lorry sent to pick up the local Hoppers and this would transport us to the farm where we would pick hops all day and be brought back home again in the evening. Later on we got down there by catching the Hoppers' Special from London Bridge.

Patrick Connor

Cobnuts and scrumping

When we walked along the lanes in autumn we could pick cobnuts from the hedgerows which lined every road and field then. Sometimes we scrumped damson plums from somebody's orchard but often the branches were just hanging over the hedge and we could pluck them off as we passed. When a field of hops had been picked we boys were given the job of climbing the hop poles and cleaning any bits of bine from the overhead wires. We made our way, hand over hand, along the wires. It was very hard on your hands. All the fields we picked were on our side of the bridge. One day we were riding to one of the fields in a lorry which skidded straight through the bridge parapet and landed in the water underneath. Mother and everyone else in the back of the lorry were thrown out into the river. Fortunately there were some Italian prisoners of war nearby who jumped in and they ran across to rescue us from the water before pulling the lorry up the river bank. We were taken to Hastings hospital as poor Mum had a terrible gash that needed stitches. All around Bodiam station were hop fields which stretched as far as Northiam and Ewhurst. Some of them were known by name, such as Clover Field which was just behind the station.

Terry Blackman

Church Farm, Paddock Wood

I spent many years hop picking and am eighty-one now. As a boy my first farm was Bradenbury Farm, Marden, then Mainwaring's Farm, and also Little Fowle Hall Farm and Church Farm Paddock Wood. My family and I have been going to the hop festival every year so far. I live in Dagenham now.

Mr J. Waites

Fruits of the field

We Wheatley children didn't do very much picking. We were allowed to go off and play for most of the time. Johnny, my older cousin and I went around the hedgerows picking blackberries and scrumping apples and other fruit. We ate some of them as we picked and took the rest home to Mum for her to make a pudding for tea.

Bill Wheatley

Little Fowle Oast at Paddock Wood. This has now been converted to bed and breakfast accommodation and guests can sleep comfortably on what was once the roasting floor.

Ready to 'earn a bob or two…' Hoppers will recognise the bundles of faggots on the roof. ['Earn…' is a quote from a popular 1950s hopping song which 'every' Hopper knows.]

A school of Hoppers

When the war started the headmaster decided to take our whole South East London secondary school hopping as he thought it would be safer in Kent than where we were, so all the top school (that is twelve years of age and upwards) were taken down to Tonbridge in Kent. The money we earned came in handy for boosting the school funds.

E. Springall

Roger Bannister and Nick Stacey

It was at this time that Dr Roger Bannister made the headlines by running the four minute mile. It had never been done in the time before and he was famous almost overnight. There was another athlete, sprinter Nick Stacey, who was a friend of Bannister's and one weekend the two of them came down to visit the hop fields and talk to the Hoppers and help the poor. At the time of his visit we didn't know him from Adolf Hitler when he came to sit on our bin and talked to us. It was only afterwards that we found out how famous he was.

Terry Blackman

My enterprising Gran

Mum and Nan were not dirty pickers but they weren't very fast at it either. Nan was a money lender and kept her money secure in a belt around her waist, well hidden by her large white apron. Going hopping was more of a holiday for her. It was very dark on the hop fields in the evenings so after dinner the adults collected their faggots, lit a fire and sat around in the flickering firelight singing the old songs, telling stories and having an occasional drink. The farmer had built bundles of faggots into a sort of haystack in the middle of a field and whenever we wanted more wood someone would go along, climb the stack and toss down a bundle to carry back to the huts.

Bill Wheatley

Measure for measure

When the measurers came round we used to keep an eye on them because some were more generous than others. The generous ones filled the bushel basket as the hops were scooped up but the miserly ones packed the basket tightly, taking more hops than was a fair measure for all our hard work.

Terry Blackman

So near and yet so far

We had a large family. Well you can imagine the size of the task to get six children up, dressed, fed and watered and all ready to go with our food packed to take with us for the day and be at the meeting place in time to catch the lorry at about 7.00 a.m. each morning. When we got home after a days work Mother had to wash, feed us and get us all off to bed. This went on for about five weeks' duration. It was a nightmare for my darling mum so dad came up with the idea of living in a Hopper's hut on the farm, to which Mum readily agreed, even though we were local pickers and not down from London. It was a perfect solution.

Patrick Connor

Bad habits started early

It was when we first went Hopping that I bought my first packet of fags. I bought 'Four for a Friend' and my brother bought a box of 'Craven A'. Gran used to send us into the village to buy her half an ounce of Wilson's snuff and when she took some it left a brown ring at the end of her nose. My mum was a powerful, stocky, peasant type of woman; very strong. When the bin got really full it sank into the mud and she'd go on one end and lift it up but it took four or five of us on the other end to lift it clear of the ground and up the rack.

Terry Blackman

Running wild

My mum tended to be constipated and had some tablets to cure her of the problem so she had to take them with her when we went down hopping. They looked like sweets and my younger brother, Tony, discovered them on the journey and couldn't resist eating them. They obviously worked very well because Mum had to dig little holes for him to sit over and use all the way down to Paddock Wood.

Bill Wheatley

Boys up to mischief

We hopped at Bodiam in the Guinness Gardens. One day we got into a field down the railway line from our hop huts. There was a herd of cows and we thought it would be great fun to get them to walk along the line. We persuaded them through a gap in the fence and they went after a bit of trouble. We never thought what would happen if a train came along. Little boys don't think that far ahead.

Terry Blackman

Gipsies and my brother Alfie

We used to have a lot of gipsies come down picking at the Bodiam farms as well. One time I saw something that was rather violent when there was a really bad fight between two gipsies. I can tell you – never watch a fight between gipsies, especially women, but there again that's how life used to be. I can remember many, many times when we were young my brother Alf would disappear. He used to have a bad leg. Mum used to go out shouting for him 'Come on! Come on, Alfie! Let's get these hops picked', especially when there were a lot of leaves to be got out because that was our job, to get the leaves out of the bin before the measurer got to us. But where was Alfie? Up in a tree. 'Come down at once Alfie!' Not him! So you can probably guess what happened to Alfie when he eventually came down.

Freddie Ganny

A near disaster

At first we picked in the gardens around Bodiam station. There were hop fields stretching as far as Northiam and Ewhurst. We were taken down by lorry to do the picking in some of the more distant fields and one morning when we were on our way to a field we'd never picked before, there was a nasty accident when our lorry skidded straight through the bridge parapet. Mother and everyone else in the back of the lorry were thrown out into the river. It was our good luck that Italian prisoners of war were working nearby and they ran across to rescue us from the water before pulling the lorry up the river bank.

Terry Blackman

David Palmer's family from Bexhill-on-Sea picking in the early twentieth century.

The first hop picking machines were huge affairs. This one, on Larkins farm, was the size of three garages end to end. These are the 'teeth' which picked the hops off the bine.

Special school form

I was allowed off school for two weeks from age 5-15 years from the middle of August every year to go hopping with my mother, Rose. A special form was issued by the schools in the ORE area for children, allowing them to be away from school. It was recognised that the children's winter clothing was paid for by the money parents earned by hop picking.

George D. Blackman

Gipsies at work

At one field we went to there were gipsies. They kept to themselves down the end of the field so we didn't have a lot to do with them. On that particular farm they used a hop-picking machine. At the front end were gipsies feeding bines into the threshing end, while at the other end were more gipsies picking out the leaves that had escaped the mechanical wire 'fingers'.

Terry Blackman

Dad built us a kitchen to be proud of

We stayed in a Hopper's hut and picked hops at Dundle Farm at Kippings Cross, Kent. In those days it was owned by a Mr Frank Swain and it worked perfectly for us. My dad and his friend built a corrugated iron kitchen fitted with a proper cast-iron stove outside the hut where Mum was able to prepare all our meals. These tasted mighty good, what with Mum being one of the old fashioned cooks. She did all the proper preparation, none of it was bought already peeled or anything, and she made delicious meat pies, fresh vegetables, apple and blackberry pies and the like. No worry about cholesterol in those days.

Patrick Conner

Above: *A hop-picking machine at Little Halden Farm.*

Right: *John Hilder's Little Halden Farm, Rolvendon.*

Scratched arms

If women were wearing short-sleeved dresses they often wore thick lisle stockings on their arms to protect them from being scratched by the bines.

Adele Coles

Policing the hop fields

In the old days I was a policeman and lived at Collier Street near Yalding. I didn't like some of the things some of the Hoppers got up to and it was my job to keep an eye on them and see they didn't misbehave. Some of the country shops put up false fronts to stop London Hoppers from stealing their goods.

Things were bad at times, and one night two pub licensees were both stabbed.

The city women were often frightened of the dark and when they had to go down the unlit country lanes at night they used to walk home arm in arm for protection as they had to pass between the dark hedgerows with bats and things scuttling about.

The police in Kent were sent down to the hopping area a month or so before picking was due to start and were mainly single men. This let them get to know the local folk so they could tell them from the Hoppers. They'd be down there for anything up to a month after the picking. Our main problem was general control over the pickers who were in their thousands, especially when they first arrived and when they left as they all arrived at different times and on different days and some stayed a couple of weeks while others stayed up to around two months as they went potato and fruit picking after the hops were finished.

We had to keep a sharp eye out for stolen property which was brought down from London and sold secretly in the hop fields. The thieves carried their loot on lorries or vans. One road to

19

*Early morning oasts.
Pen and ink sketch by
the author.*

watch was along Seven Mile Lane which was a well-known thieves' escape route.

Harry Golding

Last of a kind

John Hilder of Little Halden Farm at Rolvenden near Tenterden, is the last Kent hop farmer to still dry his hops using anthracite in his kilns.

John Liddell

Veins of gold

I can remember how cold it was early in the mornings when we went to the gardens. We always took a flask of hot cocoa and a baked potato to keep us warm. The thing I remember most vividly during hop picking was my father being responsible for drying the hops up at the oasts. At that time, the fires in the oast house were fuelled by huge lumps of coal and needed to be watched day and night to maintain the correct temperature, ensuring the hops didn't burn or were not too green. He used candle-length sticks of sulphur and there was a memorable, cloying smell as they were heated in a special pan in the furnace while the hops were drying. When we children picked up the large lumps of coal we could see veins of gold and thought we would make our fortune but the adults did not seem at all interested when we told them about it.

Adele Coles

Picking at Robertsbridge

I could tell some hopping stories! My family and I moved to the small village of Salehurst near Robertsbridge in 1953-'54. I was asked to go hop picking for a local farmer. The other pickers were all local people. We picked hops from early morning until late afternoon for four pence a bushel. At the end of three or four weeks we had earned about £20. We had fun and laughter with the farmer's family and the local families who were picking. It was not always sunny weather. We had freezing mornings; wet mornings. As you stood in the rain your boots and bins would get stuck in the mud as you tried to pull the hops but although the work was hard we still all looked forward to pay day. That was when everyone got dressed up in clean clothes to go to the farm pay office before going on the bus into Hastings for a day's shopping with the money they had subbed.

Ivy King

Our brave pilots

They grew hops on Mr Baker's Manor Farm, Laddingford and my family picked there during the war. I can remember when the V1 rockets were flying in from Germany. We were picking hops in the fields and we could see our lads flying overhead in Spitfires and they'd fly straight at the pilot-less V1s, which were jet propelled, then come up under the rockets and use their own aircraft wings to tip the rocket wing so it went off balance and crashed in the fields rather than letting them get as far as London. We admired the pilots as it was very dangerous work and they were brave lads.

Jack Chambers

Hop-flavoured tea

We picked at Greatness Farm in Sevenoaks and Mitchell's Farm in Stone Street. They were owned by a family called Hadley. When you went out picking in the fields you had to boil a kettle on a fire if you wanted to make the tea for a morning break or lunch and everything you ate tasted of hops.

Patricia Bathurst née Chatfield

Picking for Guinness's

We were day pickers at Guinness Hop Farms at Bodiam, travelling from ORE by a lorry hired from G. Booth & Sons who also collected the filled hop pokes every day and delivered them to the oasts. Then they collected the pickers for their return journey. It was a long day. We left home at 6.30 a.m. and worked until 4.00 p.m. each day excluding Saturdays when we finished at midday. I hated mornings picking for my Mum as the hops were soaking wet with dew until about 9.00 a.m. Instead, I collected all the ladies' billycans, filled them with water and lit a fire for the 9.00 a.m. tea break. Each billy had a small piece of chestnut left to float among the tea leaves, as this was said to stop the smoke spoiling the taste of the tea. I was very popular with all the ladies for doing this chore as, if left to their own devices, they would be wasting valuable picking time. Faggots for the fire were provided in a huge stack over the road by Guinness's, not far from the permanent hop huts.

George D. Blackman

Sussex hop pickers

My family picked hops at Harts Green Farm in Westfield in the 1920s. All the hops from this farm were dried out at the oast on another farm. At Harts Green there were usually three men with hop dogs (which were strong hooks on long poles; they looked like the old soldier's halberds) who went round pulling down the bines after they had been cut down ready for picking. The men usually lifted the heavy bines into the bins for us.

Mrs D. Isaac

Dodging the bats on my nightly walk

Once each day in the evenings my mother sent Dad a cooked hot dinner on a tin plate, with another upside down on top to keep it hot. I had to walk with it about a quarter of a mile from our house, along the forstall to the farm. By then it was dusk and my worst fear was the bats that flew silently through the evening sky at that time of night. They would swoop and dive, just missing me as I walked. I had heard it rumoured that they could get caught in your hair if they got close enough and I was terrified this would happen to me. At the same time I was worried about spilling or dropping Dad's precious meat meal. During daytime the walk seemed no distance at all but at night it seemed to take forever. First I had to pass the darkened cowsheds, then the rustling haystacks, then the dark water of the pond until I finally rounded the corner to the oast house, pulled back the big hop pocket which hung over the open door frame to help keep the temperature high, then, as I walked in, the oppressive heat and light of the fires hit me. I would give my dad his dinner with the feeling that I had just escaped from some dreadful danger. I stayed to watch him enjoy his one home cooked meal of the day then had to set off back the way I'd just come with his knife, fork and empty plate, all the way back home. Fortunately, without the precious dinner to carry, I could run and dodge the bats until I was safely back in our kitchen. Mother would then say 'Come on, Adele, it's time for bed'. As this was wartime most people were worried about dodging bombs, but for me it was dodging the bats!

Adele Coles

Bombing raids over Yalding

Our family went hop picking in September, then, when that was finished, we'd go on to pick fruit. We even went during the war and I can remember us all hiding in the underground dug-out which was on the edge of the field. We'd run in there when there was an air raid because we were all frightened when the heavy bombers came over from Germany: Dorniers. They had a strange broken sound to the engines so we always knew it was them.

In East Farnley near Yalding there is a grave with a memorial cross to honour the hop pickers killed in nearby fields during the war. The church holds an annual service in their memory. Opposite the station there are still some hop huts standing.

Peggy Farrant née Carter

'I want my money back!'

For years we went to Bill Page's farm off Iden Green not far from Hawkhurst. It was great. We loved going down there. My mum came down to the farm of a weekend and picked with us. There was a butcher at Tenterden who used to come round to the hop gardens bringing meat to sell to the Hoppers and Mum sometimes bought a piece from him for a stew. One year she bought a joint and when she got it back to the huts she saw it was bad. She was really annoyed and said she was going to get her hard-earned money back. She had to walk all the way from the other side of Benenden to Tenterden to return it and that was well over six miles. When she got to the shop she flung open the door and threw the meat at the butcher. 'Selling me rotten meat!' she told him, 'I want my money back!' And she made such a fuss in front of the other customers that he gave it to her, too. During the war two planes crashed on the Common and made huge craters in the ground. They sent the Home Guard round to secure them.

Joseph James

My father worked in the oast

Once they were lit, the oast fires were monitored twenty-four hours a day, so Father lived in the hot oast for a good fortnight when the drying was on, sleeping when he could on straw-stuffed sacks resting on a roughly-made wooden frame for a bed.

Adele Coles

Not everyone enjoyed hopping!

My family mostly went hopping at Eridge near Tunbridge Wells but over the years we hopped right across Kent in different gardens. My children really hated hopping but I loved it and looked forward to it every year.

Babs Wood

Settling in

When we arrived at the farm we all climbed off the lorry and got our possessions together. Mum said we should look for hut number 104. I rushed off looking at all the roughly painted numbers on each hut and soon found 104. The huts were terraced in blocks of ten or so. They were made of timber and corrugated iron with bare cement floors and each was about 12ft square. We dragged our possessions to outside the front of the hut and Mum got down to work making the place habitable.

First she laid out the faggots on the hut floor to make a base for the bed. Next she broke open the bales of straw and started pushing it into a palliasse made from two sheets stitched together down both sides and one end to form an envelope. This straw-filled palliasse was our mattress and it went on top of the faggots. We put blankets on top of it to make up our bed to sleep on. Mum swept away all the remaining straw, moved the hopping box into the hut, then carefully unpacked the oil lamp, saucepans, frying pan and teapot before making a fire so we could all settle down to a nice cup of tea and a jam sandwich. Tea never tasted so nice as that made on a fire when we were down hopping.

David Taylor, MBE

Loading the pokes to be taken by lorry to the oast at Delf's Farm, Benendon.

A childhood dream

I never owned a bike. We couldn't afford it. We'd watch from the corner as all the other boys went cycling off to the Boys' Club camp but without our own bikes we couldn't go. Despite this I had a wonderful childhood although most of the time we lived on the financial edge. We children felt like we were under the wings of a bird – protected by loving parents and family. My mum wore big black boots as they lasted longer than shoes. We had two Anderson shelters in the garden because we were such a large family. One of them was always filling with water when it rained but if it was wet when there was an air raid we all crowded into the dry one. Mum kept up a constant supply of hot cocoa all through the night during air raids to help us keep warm at night.

Terry Blackman

Diddled by Woolworths

When we got paid at the end of the season's picking I would spend most of my money buying winter clothes for my children, then we would go into Woolworths where they had a tea room in those days. One year I had £1 left. My husband said 'Go on, buy something for yourself for a change'. I wanted a bowl of hyacinth bulbs. There were two prices. The cheapest one was 8s 6d and the better one was 12s and 6p. I could not afford to waste money so went for the 8s and 6d bowl with my hard-earned £1 which I handed to the cashier expecting to get 11s and 6d change. But the cashier, who was not English, only gave me change for a 10s-note. 'I gave you a pound' I said. 'No madam, I'm sorry. You only gave me 10s' she said. When I protested she called for help. The supervisor who came believed her story and not mine. I nearly cried. That happened fifty years ago but I still think of how many hops I picked for that 10s I lost. Come on Woolworths, with fifty years' interest on ten shillings you owe me a lot of money!

Ivy King

2 The Hoppers' Railway

Bodiam Castle; a welcome sight to newly-arrived Hoppers.

When the Kent and East Sussex Railway line from Robertsbridge to Bodiam first opened in 1900 the surrounding area was full of gardens producing a constant supply of hops for the Guinness breweries. Gazing across the countryside, all the eye could see were rows of 25ft-high chestnut poles topped with wires and stringing, adorned with flowering bines exuding the rich, heady aroma of hops. Now, there are few hop growers in the area and where fruitful bines once filled the gardens which headed across the horizon there are only empty fields and a few chestnut poles leaning against the walls of picturesque, converted oast houses. Even livestock are scarce after the BSE disaster and only relatively recently are cattle and sheep back grazing the land. In a weekend of nostalgia, the

Kent and East Sussex Railway annually resurrect the Hoppers' Run from Tenterden to Bodiam where visitors celebrate with a time-honoured evening of songs and a country supper round the cheerful camp fire after spending two days hopping at a nearby farm. This popular revival of the railway's connection with Hoppers is largely thanks to two ex-hop picking sisters, Pam and Sheila Stevens, who were keen to ensure that the old hopping traditions were not lost forever. Local beer from the Rother Valley Brewery fills folks' glasses as the night crackles with sparks from burning logs. A pungent aroma of hops and wood smoke fills the air as folk exchange hopping stories while keeping an eye on potatoes baking in the embers. This is as near as it can get to the real thing.

Guinness's Railway

My father-in-law was a hop factor at Calverts Buildings. He mediated between the hop growers and the buyers. The Guinness railway taking Hoppers to the hop gardens was first opened in 1910. Their main brewery in England was the Park Royal in London, which closed in April 2004.

John Liddell

Transporting the Hoppers

The early morning Hoppers' Special brought everyone down from London Bridge and they changed at Robertsbridge where the Kent and East Sussex Railway supplied six coaches for the passengers and two green parcel vans for the special train down to the hop gardens. Railway luggage vans took all the hopping boxes and baggage. Some 10 per cent got off at Northiam, but the bulk of Hoppers dismounted at Junction Road Halt and 40 per cent went on to Bodiam.

John Miller

The Bumper

We used to wait for the farmer's letter to arrive in early September. The train running us to the gardens was known as 'The Bumper' and it went from Grove Park in South East London down to Guinness's. There were few lorries or cars on the roads in those days so we boys used to push the hopping barrow up to the station. After climbing on the train with all our baggage at Grove Park we were taken to Robertsbridge. We were lucky because Mum had friends called the Mooneys. They were a big family who all worked on the railway and could get privilege tickets for travelling, so they gave us tickets for the adults, then Mother would hide some of us behind her skirts if the inspector came round as the tickets would have cost a lot for all of us. The Bumper was very slow moving and we had plenty of time to look out the window and see the changing scenery.

Terry Blackman

Britain's first light railway, the Kent and East Sussex, still runs its trains regularly between Tenterden and Bodiam.

Calverts Buildings, London. Hop factors. (Courtesy of Larkins Brewery)

The Hoppers' reunion

When Bodiam station was re-opened by railway enthusiasts in 2000 we were surprised to see so many elderly people visiting the site. They didn't seem to be quite as interested in our large collection of railway engines and rolling stock so much as in the station itself. After a while, our curiosity was aroused and we asked, what was their interest in the station? 'We're ex-hop pickers here on a nostalgic visit to the area where we used to pick. All around here were Guinness's farms. Sadly, the station is now the only place left that is still recognisable and to which we can relate. Everything else – most of the fields, the Guinness hop farms, the old huts, everything we knew so well after coming down here for many years, has gone.' When we heard this, the germ of an idea was formed and our enthusiasts decided to give the Hoppers a taste of the past. We went into the history of what part the Robertsbridge to Bodiam railway line had played in Guinness's hop growing and brewing past and in September 2002 held a hop pickers' reunion at Bodiam station, where we have two Hoppers' huts and a hop garden of our own. The event was keenly supported by the Hoppers themselves and for two days the station and camping field were inundated with enthusiastic ex-Hoppers eager to meet old friends and talk over their reminiscences. It has now become an annual event.

John Miller

Kent and East Sussex Railway signal box at Tenterden Town.

A Kent and East Sussex Railway train negotiating a bend on the line between Tenterden and Bodiam.

John Miller lights the open fire for an evening cuppa.

Bodiam station waiting room. (Courtesy of Iain Ross-McLeod)

Hiding from the ticket inspectors

When we first used to come here we had to go to Robertsbridge and get off, then from Robertsbridge we used to get the train to Bodiam and we called that The Bumper Line for some unknown reason, or the Tin Lizzie. Many things used to happen there and we used to find ourselves hidden under the seats, on top of the rack and you can make your own conclusion as to why we were put there if you like! I had to tell you about that because it was so funny to have to do it. If no-one was looking we had great fun going on what we called an engine type of thing with four wheels and two handles at each end and we used to run it up and down the line until we were chased off.

Freddie Ganny

The Hoppers' friends

Huxfords hosed down their coal lorries in August and carried all us Hoppers and our heavy luggage down to the hop camps, particularly Northlands. There were eight Hopping camps around the Guinness's farms at Clovers Field and Junction Halt. Guinness's was split into seventeen sub-farms. There was a mobile cinema that went from camp to camp and they advertised their programme and the rural bus timetable beforehand in the local free newspaper at St Dunstan's every September so we knew what was coming. They showed the same films at each camp. The railway closed in 1961.

Two coaches came down and one parcel van at the weekends. They brought our husbands, friends and any other members of the family

Hoppers' train at Bodiam station. (Courtesy of Iain Ross-McLeod)

Engine 32678 at Robertsbridge with a Hoppers' train for Bodiam. Engine 1012 is passing, right, with more Hoppers from Hastings. September 1957.

Steam train at Bodiam station, Sussex.

Ex-Hoppers enjoying a brew-up with John Miller at the Bodiam Hop Festival.

Boris, Banjo and ex-Hoppers on their way to Bodiam Castle, 10 June 2003.

who wanted to come. Mostly they were the men who were working at their jobs through the week so could only do their picking at the weekends. They brought down extra clothes and food supplies with them.

John Liddell

'The train now arriving at Junction Road station… '

When the train arrived from Robertsbridge to either Junction Road or Bodiam stations it was longer than the platform and several carriages did not have anywhere for passengers to step out, so we children jumped down and no one noticed us as we slipped through the fence. Lorries came to take our hopping boxes and other baggage and gave us lifts to our field. We were in the Clover Field which was just behind the station. When I was eleven I had just won a scholarship to go to Colfe's when we went off hop picking and it meant I was late going back

Ford railmotor set No. 1 soon after delivery in 1923. This was known as 'The Bumper'.

to school. I was really embarrassed having to explain to the teacher why I was starting several days later than the other boys as none of them went hopping and most people looked down on Hoppers as very poor people.

Terry Blackman

The important role of the railway

In the later years of hop growing, Guinness's arranged for lorries to meet pickers at Northiam and Bodiam stations. These were owned by Huxfields Coal Merchants who had depots at both these places. The lorries were full of coal dust so were very dirty. Huxfields usually washed them down before meeting the Hoppers arriving at the stations, then carried the hopping boxes, elderly and very young Hoppers to their hop huts in nearby fields. The able ones walked along the roads which were quite safe as most of the traffic at the time consisted of horses and carts. If the trains arrived shortly after Huxfields had been making coal deliveries and there wasn't time to wash them down, the lorries would do the same job but still had coal dust in them. The Hoppers expected to stay at the hop farms from five to six weeks according to that particular year's abundance of crops.

Guinness paid for the new station at Bodiam, a siding which was built in 1910 as it was needed by them for all their goods deliveries, in particular, 'shoddy'. This was shredded material, ends, from wool and cotton textile mills which was put in holes dug to plant the hops. This helped to retain moisture in the earth for the plants. Once rotted, being a natural material, it became a kind of fertilizer. This is the original meaning of 'shoddy', now used to refer to badly-manufactured goods. The railway was also needed to carry sacks of fertilizer, chemicals to treat the bines as well as shop goods. As the hops were processed and dried they were packed in large sacks called pockets. At nearby Court Lodge Farm the hop pockets were loaded up and brought by tractor to Bodiam station then sent by train up to the hop factors in Borough High Street near London Bridge station. Guinness had a total of 1,400 acres used for dairy farming and a mixed farm of pasture and arable. Of these, 800 or more acres were cultivated for growing hops for their brewery.

John Miller

3 Rother Valley Brewery

The Rother Valley Brewery, Hop and Dairy Farm in Northiam has the advantage of being close to picturesque Bodiam Castle and the Kent and East Sussex border. It is known locally as Gate Court Farm and supplies nearby villagers with their morning milk and fresh produce. However it is also a successful brewery with its own working hop farm now growing a newly developed variety of English hop: the Boadicea, developed by Wye College near Ashford in Kent. Beer is brewed at Rother Valley in the traditional way without the use of imported or pelletised hops and the brewery has developed its own special yeast for the fermentation process. The result is a selection of highly drinkable, natural tasting porters and mellow beers. The business has four working directors; Stephen Leman, Peter and John Cyster who own the dairy and hop farm, and Colin Smith who, as the head brewer, is responsible for the running of the brewery. New crowns of Boadicea were planted in October, 2003 and these will be trained up netting rather than the usual stringing. When deciding in which direction to plant the hop rows it is more important to sow the field in such a way that the machine can pick in long runs rather than referring to the direction of the sun or wind. A bulky mechanical picker does not like having to turn too many corners, nor work across the side of a hill as its height and weight would cause it to topple over, so hops are planted in such a way as to avoid this. The hop is a hardy plant. The roots grow down to a depth of six feet or so and, depending on the variety, weather and growing conditions, can last up to forty years or more so each garden planted is an investment in potential.

Stephen Lehman and Colin Smith. (Courtesy of Iain Ross-McLeod)

Machine picking

Brewing is a futures market as so much money has to be put up front for capital investment. This is difficult to assess as there is no way of accurately predicting the cost of hops or production in four years' time. We largely grow our own hops but buy them in too. Rother Valley Brewery bought a picking machine ten years ago in 1993. This was developed in Germany and is much smaller and neater than earlier types. Now we pick hops by machine directly from bines growing in the field. It comprises a tractor with the picking machine offset behind it so it can pick on both sides of the bines at once. Hops are gathered up into a funnelled collector and dropped into a trailer

The author and Peter Cyster loading Boadicea Hop Crowns ready for planting. (Courtesy of Iain Ross-McLeod)

following behind. At one time we employed 400 pickers; now we only need twenty. Only two men are required to work the picking machine. When we first bought it the cost was £50,000. A new, similar one nowadays would cost £35,000. Hops now grow up wire or plastic netting, finding their own way rather than being twiddled up stringing. This is called 'easy care hop farming'. Before, it would have cost us £1,000 an acre. It would have been £150 an acre just to do the stringing. Now we can do it for less.

Stephen Leman, Rother Valley Brewery Director

Britain's new Boadicea

We cultivate about twenty acres of hops at 3,000 hop plants to an acre. Two years ago (2001) Wye College developed a new strain of hop called Boadicea which we now grow. It has the advantage of being an organic hop only growing to 10ft tall. Boadicea only requires an occasional manuring and is a particularly useful variety as it is strongly resistant to mildew – a major problem of hop growing – as well as blight, other diseases and aphids. Aphids are grubs of the damsel fly

which arrive in July and they can sweep through a crop like wildfire, but the leaves of Boadicea are too bitter for them. There are also red spiders. We can't prevent them but get round the problem by importing a special variety of African spider to control them. These are so small you can hardly see them and they can't 'fly' like other spiders, but we scatter a few handfuls among the bines and they gobble up all the red spiders before dying off in the winter. We buy more for next year's crop. An added advantage of Boadicea is that there is a shorter inter-nodal growth on the bines than on taller varieties. This means that as there is less stem between bunches of hops we get more to the bine. The first time we grew Boadiceas we trained them up plastic netting but it didn't last the season so we're going back to using string.

Peter Cyster, farmer and Rother Valley Brewery Director

The brewing process

Rother Valley produces four cask beers and three bottled beers. Our main beer is called *Level Best* which is 4 per cent alcohol. We also produce

Rother Valley Brewery. Mash tun.

Tenterden and *Boadicea*, which are hop beers, *Hopper's Ale* and *Blues* which are both cask and bottled beers and the 3.7 per cent alcohol *Wealdon Bitter*. We mainly use Phoenix as our bittering hop. These are boiled for sixty minutes to start off with. East Kent Goldings and others are used for flavouring. Goldings have a sweeter, more mellow smell than Phoenix. Crushed malt is put into the hopper which in turn sends it through an Archimedes screw to the hop crusher or mash tun. The resulting wort falls down into a copper regulated by a flow valve. It travels through a cold water tank and lastly, the cold break vat set at approximately 20° where the yeast and fixings are added. After an hour's fermentation in the vat or tun the proteins drop out and the yeast raises a head on the beer. Yeast is a type of live fungus which self-generates and is kept from one brew to the next. The residue of mash is fed to our cattle.

Colin Smith, Rother Valley Head Brewer
and Director

Workers from abroad

We come regularly from Bulgaria to England to work and have worked on Gate Court Farm for several years. We plant the new hop plants approximately two feet apart down the rows. Here is good soil, easy to dig on this farm. Working here we learn many things about growing and farming hops. Our families grow hops in Bulgaria. Ilyan's father owns a hop farm there. This is good work here. Peter Cyster has brought us yoghurts and I like them to eat.

Pelar Chovalski, Ivan Vlaev, Iliyan Ivanov

Bulgarian workers at Gate Court Farm. (Courtesy of Iain Ross-McLeod)

4 The Bountiful Bine

All the family joined in with the picking.

Most hop pickers can recall their first impressions on seeing the hop fields; of walking down Kent and East Sussex country lanes as the sun rose, its orb hazed by the early morning dew, while raucous rooks flew among their untidy nests before swooping down on the fields to find the first meal of their day. On either side, cobnut hedges flourished, protecting row upon row of high hop poles and strings up which grew hop-laden bines ripe for the picking. A heady, pungent aroma of hops filled the air, bees and other insects buzzed in the sunlight while a choir of thrushes, blackbirds, robins and other songbirds sang a near-deafening cacophony of their dawn chorus – sounds seldom heard nowadays, sadly. Spider webs filled fox-forced gaps in hedgerows, stretching from twig to twig while dewdrops traced their shape like sparkling

diamonds. Occasionally a pheasant darted across the road right under your feet and, in the open fields, rabbits played largely unaware of their danger from small, hungry London boys keen to add them to the family stew pot for dinner that night. This was paradise; where a child could stuff his pockets with a lump of bread, a piece of cheese, help himself surreptitiously to an apple as he passed the farmer's orchard and stay out all day in a land where he could climb trees, paddle in a stream, catch tiddlers or sticklebacks in a jam jar, spend a day of serendipity and return home to the hop fields and his family safely and without a care in the evenings, satisfied his day had been well spent. This existence was a total contrast to how many normally lived in the dingy London back streets that were home.

Sid, Nora, Maud, Joan and Mrs Poile's Mum hop picking pre-war.

Maurice Sargent as a pole puller in September 1953.

My first day as a poke boy

I arrived at the farm promptly at 7.00 a.m. which was when I had been told my working day would start. I was full of excitement at the prospect of starting my first proper job but at the same time was apprehensive as to whether or not I could do it. I need have had no worries; I was taken under the wing of the Head Wagoner who proved to be a great tutor as well as a good friend to me, new as I was to the job. My duties entailed helping with any of the tasks in the hop garden, such as moving the heavy sacking and pole 'bins' into which the hops were picked, helping to pull bines down which the pickers found too tough to pull on their own and even cutting them down from the overhead wires. I also had to distribute the pokes, or special sacks, and make sure there was one ready beside each bin. Pokes are big hessian sacks about 6ft long and 4 ft wide; each held ten bushels of freshly picked hops with plenty of room to spare to avoid them from being crushed.

Roger Jeffries

Al fresco lunches

Our lunches were bread, cheese and tomatoes with mugs of hot tea which we ate out in the fields. Our fingers were stained yellow by the hops. No food or cuppa has ever since come near to such perfection. They were my happiest childhood memories. Sadly, later on, only university students were taken on to hook up the bines on the new mechanical machines. My mother and friends had lost a way of life that they loved. The machines never picked as meticulously as the hand pickers, who were not allowed to pick leaves into the bins when the measurer arrived. Several unemployed men were employed as pole pullers. They pulled down hop heads which had been left up on the wires, using long poles with a special hook to snap off the heads. All loose hops on the ground had to be picked up as they were too valuable to waste. I remember trains collecting the pokes on open trucks from Northiam station which was only opened for the Hop season. They were sent up to London for processing.

George D. Blackman

Those early mornings

It was always misty and dewy when the dawn came up and that was when we were getting ready to go out picking. Mum lit the fire and made us all a cup of tea and a breakfast of bread and jam before we set off. Everything was soaking wet from the dew. The bins were of the traditional kind and we needed two for our family. Mother, me, Gran, Pat and the little twins had one bin between us and the rest had a second bin. The bin was placed so that it was between four hop sets, or plants, with one at each corner. This made them easier to reach. First we took off the leaves, then swept our hands along the bine to swipe off the hops using the crook of our thumb and first finger. It made your hands sore. The farmer was fussy that we left the overhead wires and bin area completely clear once the bines were down and we had to pick up any hops we dropped, pile the leaves up and coil the used bines once they had been cleared and leave them neatly by the set. Our family were all very quick pickers and the bin was often overflowing well ahead of the measurer coming round to tally it. One chap stood at the end of the bin holding the sacks open, ready, while the measurer stood next to him and bent down into the bin with his basket, scooping the hops into it with a sweep of his arm and counted each bushel into the pokes. When these were full they were tied off and stacked to one side of the drift ready for a horse and cart to collect them for the oast house.

Terry Blackman

Early mornings and welcome breaks

Mum used to get us up in the mornings very early and we would have a quick wash, get dressed then have our breakfast. We children would then go off down to the hop gardens at about 7.30 a.m. to start picking and Mum would join us at about 8.30 a.m. after preparing sandwiches, cakes and other welcome morsels, vacuum flasks filled with tea and bottles full of made-up squash all ready to be consumed by six very hungry children during various breaks in the day. Mum would then leave the hop garden at about 4.00 p.m. to go back to the hut and prepare our evening meal.

Patrick Conner

That all-important letter

Everybody got a letter. Without the letter you couldn't go hopping. Once that brown envelope came through the door we knew we could go on holiday. The farmer could only contact us by letter because hardly anyone could afford their own telephone in those days. When there was an emergency most people had to use the public telephones out in the street. Mobile phones hadn't been invented. Hopping started in September and could last from three to four weeks. Sometimes, after the hop picking was finished, a friend of my mother's used to take us fruit picking at Wateringbury.

Terry Blackman

First hopping

I have happy memories of my first day in the hop fields. We sat in the back of an open lorry one morning at dawn. It left our little market town behind and carried us through the September morning mists. I was eight years old, wedged between Mother and Gran, watching the road spew out behind us like a great escalator. 'Hold tight and sit still!' Mother admonished. I listened to the women chattering around me. Some had babies on their laps and toddlers at their knee. The road narrowed, we turned in to a leafy lane and for the first time I smelled the tang of

Hilda and Measurer with a bushel basket, loading pokes onto the lorry for delivery to Delphs Farm's oast house.

autumn woods. I thought it must have been like that on the first day of the world.

Mrs D. Boreham

A stormy night to remember

There was a terrible disaster one year when the weather was really stormy and travelling was dangerous on the roads. It was raining heavily and the roads were wet underfoot. The poor old dray horse pulling a cartload of Hoppers down to the hop gardens lost his footing on the slippery boards when crossing a bridge and fell into the river below. Everyone was drowned.

Val Nokes

Pole pulling at Guestling and Icklesham

I lived in Woodside Chapel Lane, Guestling and we picked hops in the Guestling and Icklesham areas where hop gardens were numerous in the 1900s. In late August and through September the buses used to go past our house to Pett and Fairlight, full up with people going to pick at Merricks Farm in Icklesham. Special buses were run out and back every day for two or three weeks according to the season. In the 1950s we

worked for Coopers of Stocks Green Farm at Guestling. Merricks was a much bigger farm than Stocks where I usually worked. We always hoped for a dry spell at that time of year as picking wet hops was very unpleasant with the water running down your arms and under your collar. I was a pole puller and in the photo I am smoking a cigarette [see pg. 36] but I never smoked much, then or since. It was thought to be sophisticated to be a smoker in those days so someone gave me a cigarette for when I had my picture taken. Some of my hopping photos date back to the late 1800s.

Each pole puller had about nine bins to look after, moving them around from drift to drift then on to another area when that part was all picked. If you happened to have a band of quick pickers you moved quickly through the garden and then doubled back when you reached the end and went to help the slower ones.

Maurice Sargent

Clean up before leaving the bins

Mum stopped picking at around 4.00 p.m. and walked back to our hop huts to get dinner ready. We children usually stayed until about 4.30 p.m. but for some time after because we were still picking and clearing up around the hop bins before returning to the hop hut. This was because everything had to be left clean ready to start picking the next day and we were expected to clear up round our own bins.

Patrick Conner

Unusual hopping huts

Our huts were built in twos and we each had our own fire, unlike Hoppers on many other gardens who had to share cooking facilities. The two rooms in the huts faced in opposite directions so that each family's room was quite private and our door faced one way towards our fire and the adjoining room faced the other way. We picked on Guinness's farms and on the morning we were due to go down to the farm we walked to Grove Park station to catch The Bumper train. As we walked along we were booed for being Hoppers as they thought only poor people went hopping.

Terry Blackman

Deal Farm, Peasmarsh Street

The driver changed gear roughly and we were thrown forward so he got some good-natured barracking. We bumped through the farm gates, the lorry stopped and the driver came round to help the less agile of us get down. I wanted to jump down on my own but he lifted me onto the verge. It was still heavy with dew on sparkling spiders' webs like diamante cartwheels. Bags and hopping boxes were off-loaded and we trailed into the first garden. Hops hung there like small, green fir cones, distinctly pungent.

Mrs M. Boreham

HM the Queen's Coronation

We had trouble in 1953 which is when the Queen's Coronation was on in London and required heavy policing. The police who'd been on duty in the Kent hop fields were drafted in to cover the event came in for a lot of teasing. The London police were calling out 'Here come the hop pickers!' when we arrived to go on duty. The popular

Hoppers' huts at Bodiam with the Clover Field behind.

Goldings are Kent hops and it was my family relations who first produced them. There is a smaller version now called First Gold which only grows up to twelve or so feet and is ideal for picking by today's mechanical pickers.

Harry Golding

Dad kept working during the week

Dad used to bring down all the necessary provisions at weekends as he was working all through the week. He was a manager for the Medway Coal Company in Tunbridge Wells and would come down to the farm for a couple of hours some days when he found the time in between jobs. We would have loved to have had him with us all the time but his job had to come first. I doubt if he would have had much effect on our tally when it came to the picking because he was such a slow picker. Mum used to get him to 'tail' the bines, leaving the mass of hops for her to pick because then she could, what she called, 'scratch them off' easier. I didn't consider myself a bad picker either. Like most of the other children there we would do our stint of sitting up between the bines, picking into an open, upturned umbrella or into a box so we could earn some pocket money which we got at the end of the hopping season when Mum got paid. Not that we got very much because most of it went on clothes to wear to school, or for shoes.

Patrick Conner

Dirty pickers

My gran was a dirty picker and she caused us some work because of it. She smashed her hops, leaves and anything that came off with them straight into the bin so her end of it was always full up with leaves. We children got the blame for it. The measurer often sat down after measuring our bin because he said he was worn out. When he'd gone we'd put in three or four more sacks-full that we'd already picked and kept in reserve. My sister had dermatitis and the hop juice made it worse so she always wore a pair of gloves when she was picking.

Terry Blackman

The day war broke out

As children, my sister Joan and I were told we were to be evacuated to an old couple living in Shipbourne in Kent. On the day war broke out we were sent down there. It was September and the start of the hop-picking season so we were told to join in and pick hops. We knew the other Hoppers were getting a shilling for every bushel they picked, but at the end of the week after all our hard work my sister was given a shilling and I only got sixpence.

Bill Covil

An old hop-picking film

In 1953 a children's film was shot in Goudhurst, Kent about life in the hop fields. The film was nearly lost forever when it was discarded in a skip outside a Chicago film studio. Fortunately an American film buff rescued it and offered it for sale. Barry Littlechild of Tunbridge Wells bought the film on the off-chance that it would prove worthwhile and was delighted to discover it had been filmed locally. He offered to show the film in Goudhurst and was overwhelmed by the response. Since then he has shown it many times

to capacity audiences. Now, unfortunately, it is wearing out. Some of the youthful stars of the film are Anthony Valentine, Jane Asher, Mandy Miller and Melvyn Hayes. Barry used all the money raised to support the Heart of Kent Hospice in Pembury; over £20,000. He hopes to show it many times more but it cost £300 just to replace a mere eight minutes of footage. Unless money can be found to pay for the rest of the film's revival it may well be lost to posterity. If anyone is interested in helping to save this unique record of hopping days I will put them in touch with Barry.

Hilary Heffernan

Storm in a hop field

One particular year there was a tremendous storm with strong winds which brought down all the hop poles with strings, wires and bines still attached to them. The whole area was a real mess. Our family was among those the farmer asked to pick that field and it was so difficult he gave us extra money for doing the job. We had to climb in and out of the poles and wires and the hops were wet through and stuck to our hands as we picked.

Terry Blackman

Hop huts forever

When we went there for a visit recently we were pleased to see there are ex-Hoppers' huts at Chainhurst near Yalding that are still being lived in.

Patsy Burgess

Time for tea

On the last official break before we were due to finish I was sent back down to the huts to light a fire and put on the water to boil ready to start tea. The pot was suspended from the middle of the overhead cross bar above the flames as everyone wanted a drink of tea as soon as they got back to the huts. The ladies wore double-fronted, wraparound aprons to protect their clothes and head scarves to keep the bits of bine

Village shops sold nearly everything a body could need from gas mantles and coffee to isinglass for preserving eggs, and teapots.

out of their hair. Mum always sat cross-legged on a chair and you could see her long knickers and stockings which were tied up at the top around a half penny to stop them from slipping down. Mum had a way of cutting bread that was usual then but you hardly ever see now; she tucked a loaf of bread under one arm, got a bread knife and cut upwards towards her. She had a terrible habit with cheese, holding it up in the air and slicing it off into uneven pieces onto thick slices of bread. I suppose it was to save time. We had to eat everything Mum gave us or she thought we were ill. After tea we put out the fire, tidied up and went back to picking. We walked everywhere because there were no buses. As we went towards the village mum would send two of us up ahead to the International Stores for provisions before going on to a little farm where we could get potatoes, sloes, turnips, cabbages, cobnuts and apples. There was no foreign food as there were no imports during the war and everyone had to make do with what was available in the shops. Mum started dinner about 6.00 or 7.00 p.m.

Terry Blackman

5 Larkins Brewery

Chris Howlynd's family hopping during the 1950s.

Larkins of Chiddingstone, near Edenbridge, was originally a hop farm of 200 acres owned by the Langridge family. The farm name came from Theobalden Bartholemew Lovekyn who owned the land in 1250. Bob Dockerty, the present owner, cultivated twenty acres of hops. The farm was converted to a brewery in 1989. When Larkins first started there were 250 breweries in Kent alone.

The brewery uses a wide variety of hops for their beers including Bramling Cross, Fuggles, East Kent Goldings and Sussex Martletts, names familiar to most hop pickers. Larkins now produce 2,000 casks each year which are mainly supplied to local public houses. Stainless steel kegs are used in preference to barrels as these are easier and quicker to sterilise. After a while the linings of aluminium barrels are affected by the beer and deteriorate while stainless steel casks do not suffer from this problem.

Honoured by the French

The present owner of Larkins, Bob Dockerty, recalls that it was his great grandfather, born in 1790, who established the hop farm while his grandfather, born in 1876 was made a *Chevalier d'Oublon* or Knight of the Hops in honour of his achievements in the beer industry.

The Plenum Chamber

While there are at least six conventional oast houses close to the brewery, Larkins built a large barn-like structure with a rolling horsehair mat flooring which runs across the rectangular slatted floor of the plenum★ chamber with an area twice as large as a traditional drying floor. This was known as a Jones Hetherington Roller Hop Floor. Hops were tipped evenly across the drying floor then wound across on rollers to allow more hops to be spread evenly over the floor as the first lot dried by heat from a boiler next to the drying room. A rolling gantry allowed workers to cross the floor so the hops could be inspected without being trodden on and damaged. Dried hops were wound off the matting across the other end of the room and tipped off onto the pressing floor in the next room to be collected into the usual 150 bushel pockets and rammed tightly in a hop press. As each pocket was filled close to brimming, they were removed from the press then sewn fast across the top with coping string using a large, curved coping needle with a specially flattened and shaped point to allow it to penetrate the sacking. Moisture from the drying floor escaped through a house-shaped vent positioned along the roof ridge.

★The Shorter Oxford English Dictionary defines 'plenum' as being 'a system of artificial ventilation in which fresh air, forced into the building to be ventilated, drives out the vitiated air'.

A Larkins hop pocket.

An early hop-picking machine

During the last few years of their hop growing days Larkins installed an impressive hop picking machine which runs the full length of a fifty foot purpose-built shed and is some twenty feet high in parts. Apart from being extremely noisy for the few workers required to operate it, this was representative of the kind of mechanical picker brought in to replace the armies of Hoppers who had formerly invaded Kent annually for their seasonal hop picking holiday.

To achieve the picking, freshly pulled bines are hooked onto a vertical conveyor belt which lifts them up and across the machine on a series of mechanical hooks. These lower the bine onto a bed of 275 wire hooks or pickers which extract the hops while most of the leaves and broken bine fall through to be collected and ejected. Hops then move across a flat bed with lateral hooks for removing any leaves or branches missed by the first part of the process. The last part of the machine conveys the hops to waiting ten bushel pokes where they are bagged ready for delivery to be dried in the nearby oast. This amazing machine now lies idle and is hardly worth its weight in scrap metal. It was

Larkins Brewery logo.

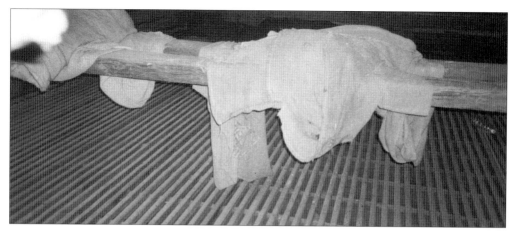

An unusual Roller Hop Floor at Larkins Brewery. This is a moving, slatted drying floor.

Larkins' furnace heater for under-floor hop drying, using the rolling hop floor.

Early hop picking-machine at Larkins. (Courtesy of Iain Ross-McLeod)

Larkins' Farm hop press. The flaps at the back open onto Larkins' roller floor.

Larkins' brewery control box for the mash tuns.

built by Bruff Engineering and installed by Drake & Fletcher of Maidstone.

From bine to beer

The brewing process is started by malt extract and water being heated in the copper before un-pocketed bittering hops are added and brought to the boil. The enzyme which converts barley into maltose is Beta Amylase. It then flows to an under back where the temperature is cooled. The malt is sparged (or sprinkled) in the mash tun before adding in aroma hops (Fuggles or Goldings). Yeast is added in the fermenter where it ferments, expanding into a heady, aromatic foam, until finally the beer is racked into stainless steel barrels or bottles and sealed ready for delivery. The yeast is creamed off ready for re-use before the racking process. The whole process takes from three days to two weeks according to the product, from start to finish.

Racking the beer at Larkins. (Courtesy of Iain Ross-McLeod)

45

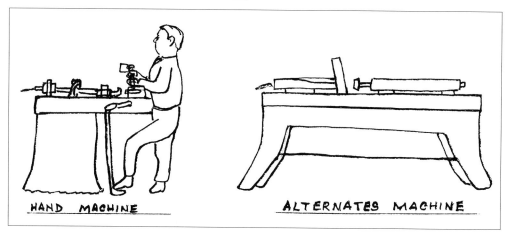

Wood turning for making shives, or bungs, for beer barrels. Drawings by George and Elsie Maddock.

Bob Dockery in the brewery office with a painting of Larkins Hop Farm.

How porter got its name

Larkins produce three different bitters through the year and a porter in September. Porter was originally made for the London porters as a rough drink but then it was improved, made smoother tasting and called 'extra stout'; in other words extra strong.

The brewer's breakfast

A fresh egg is broken into the hot mash where it quickly cooks, taking in the flavour of hops. This makes a nourishing snack and is known as the Brewer's Breakfast.

Bob Dockerty

Buildings housing the drying and bagging rooms at Larkins Brewery.

Sparls and shives

Being tapered, the bungs we made went into the barrels easily and once they soaked up the beer they made a perfect seal. When a barrel needed to be opened, a tap was fixed into a special hole on one end of the barrel and the shive in the top hole was rapped smartly, using a small wedge called a sparl. This broke away the remaining bit of wood left between the two holes and let the air in. If this wasn't done an airlock formed and the contents of the barrel wouldn't flow properly. When we had to make corks we used best black cork which came in bundles. We also made cork bath mats and table mats. Nowadays most cork things are made from cork pieces and off-cuts glued together, which is cheaper than using the sheets.

George Maddock and Elsie

We are a beer-loving nation

Amazingly, Britons drink on average around 29 million pints of beer every day of the year. No wonder Julius Caesar called it 'a high and mighty liquor'. He obviously managed to find some compensation for having landed in our cold climate!

George Green

6 Hopping Holidays

Apart from the money they could earn, hopping to Londoners meant a month down in the country living the healthy life denied them in the 'pea-souper' fogs and smoke of London. Sometimes the smog (smoke and fog) was so thick a person could not see to walk down the street. I remember as a child, bumping into the fog-shrouded post box into which I was posting a letter, because I could not see beyond my outstretched hand. It was quite terrifying to cross a road in thick smog because although cars could be heard approaching slowly, you couldn't see or hear the coming of bicycles and their riders. When smog arrived it was a good time to leave London and go on holiday to the hop fields of Kent and Sussex. Before the 1960s, hop farms mainly used five kinds of pickers and workers to harvest their crops. First were members of the farmers' own families, all roped in to do their stint once the harvest was ready and sometimes taken for granted when it came to pay day. Then there were local villagers many of whom, like the farming families, worked on the farm throughout the year and whose family members joined in when it was time for 'all hands on deck' at picking time. The next group, by far the most numerous, were the hundreds of thousands of Londoners drafted in seasonally from August to September. Fourthly were the gypsies who travelled across country with their caravans and families at the end of summer to pick hops, fruit and potatoes according to what work was available in that particular district. The fifth group were individual itinerant families who made their way across from one hop field, vegetable field and orchard to another, grateful for the work, accommodation and the chance to earn some money.

Poke boy

I left school in 1943. I was fourteen and looking for a job. Someone told me a local farmer wanted extra labour for the hopping season, helping out with harvesting the hops. I decided to apply for the job. 'Do you know anything about hops and hopping?' the farmer wanted to know. I replied 'Yes, I've been hop picking with my mother for three or four seasons and the last couple of times I had half a bin on my own'. 'Well that's a good start. We begin work at seven o'clock in the morning and work until five o'clock. It's a full-time job. The wages will be eighteen shillings a week and we pay extra for overtime. If your work and timekeeping are up to the mark there might be a job for you after the hop picking is over. We're starting next Monday so if you want the job you can start then.'

Roger Jeffries

Work in hop gardens goes on all the year round

I worked on Coopers, an East Sussex hop farm, for four years in the 1950s. It was at Guestling Thorn. We cut back all the previous year's growth on each of the bines then trimmed the roots back early in the year. When all that was finished we did the stringing on the overhead wire mesh frame at the top of the poles. The next job was training newly grown bines up the strings as they grew taller. This had to be done regularly as they developed quite fast. We shimmed (hoed) in between the rows to control the weeds as they took the goodness from the soil. When the hops were ready during August, I got the job of pole puller and bin man. This meant hooking down the bines as they were needed by the pickers and carrying them to the bins in my charge for them to pull off the hops. After being measured into pokes they were taken to the oast house for processing.

Maurice Sargent

Local labour and Londoners' holiday

The picking of hops was performed by both local inhabitants and pickers who came down from London to do the job. The latter were provided with accommodation in Hoppers' huts. These were mostly one room, often with a blanket strung across the middle for modesty if there were several people sharing a hut. It was generally regarded as a holiday by the Londoners as it got them out of the city and was a good opportunity to earn enough money to fit the children out with clothes and boots for the winter. The convenient aspect was that the money they earned was usually paid in a lump sum at the end of the picking although some pickers asked for subs or advances at the weekends while they were there. The majority of older children helped their mothers to pick hops while the younger ones played in the hop garden during their six weeks away from school. Some of the youngsters were introduced to hop picking by being given an inverted, open umbrella and sitting on the ground beside it while picking and filling it with hops. This would be tipped in with their parents' bin, thereby earning their pocket money. The highlight of their day was when the 'stop me and buy one' ice cream man came by, wearing his white coat while riding a three-wheeled refrigerated tricycle from which he sold sixpenny ices.

Roger Jeffries

Hovering the hops

The pole puller had done his work and each bin had bines lying across it ready for stripping. I had to sit on an upturned box and pick into an open umbrella. I was told that only when it was full could I go and play. I picked as fast as my small

Converted oast house near Lullingstone. The old hop drying room makes an excellent large sitting room.

fingers could go, sometimes pausing to examine tiny red spiders or a ladybird. Just before midday, Amos the tally man came round to record the number of bushels in each bin. I saw Mum pick out the leaves then 'hover' the hops, plunging her arms beneath them and lifting them up so they were not so tightly packed. I am seventy-four now, but the memories are still fresh.

Mrs D. Blackman

Helping in the home

I was born in a three-storied house in Camberwell, one of nine children; two boys and seven girls. We all had to help with the chores, bed making, cleaning the cutlery, whitening the hearth, black-leading the grate, washing up and peeling potatoes. Instead of a bathroom we had a large tin bath brought in from the garden and put in front of the fire. All hot water was boiled in saucepans on top of the cooker and the bath was emptied after two of us had bathed. One day, out of the blue, Mum said we were going hopping. Everything was packed into a trunk and the greengrocer took us down in his horse and cart. One sister sat beside him as he took us to catch The Hoppers' Special train. The train arrived at our destination very early, so we had to sleep at the station until the farm wagon came and took us to the farm where we were allocated a brick hut. Our first job was to get the faggot

Youngsters on their hopping holiday.

Pictured on a postcard

I remember the rain the most! Especially when it ran down the back of my neck as I was trying to pick hops. My husband's Mum, Susie Blaney, was in one of the hop-picking postcards and she was the oldest potato picker in Kent when she was eighty.

Kathy Powell née Smith

'...chased the girls and made them cry'

We were collected by truck in Hastings and taken to go hopping on Mr John Merrick's farm at Bodiam. The Binesman cut down the bines complete with string, then carried them over to our bin all ready to be picked. We used wood and hessian fold-up bins and also picked into bushel baskets. After the week's picking the adults liked to go to the Robin Hood Pub at Icklesham. When we were youngsters we'd chase the girls, carry them back and tip them into the hop bins!

Terry Blackman

bundles and lay them in the hut for the base of the bed before covering it with straw and more straw in pillowcases for pillows. A few yards away was the brick cookhouse. We lit a fire with sticks and hung a saucepan on the bar to make the tea.

Kathy Dennis

Romance in the Hop Fields

I was born as a result of hop picking. My mum used to stay back late in the gardens, picking hops and Dad said 'you think more of those damned hops than you do of me and getting my tea!' so she had to leave it and go back to the hop huts. As a result, I was born nine months later.

Stephanie Cater

Married to a Romany

My Mum's sister was married to a Romany, and hopped at Yalding. The Lees came from Canning Town. Mum came from Dagenham. She was nicknamed 'Rosy Apple'.

Catherine Creed

Buried treasure and Hastings lights

There were three huge craters in the meadows near where we picked. They were where German aircraft had crashed in the war. The planes are still there, buried. They flew straight into the ground. After the war we liked to stand at the top of our meadow and we could see all the lights of Hastings lit up from there at night time.

Joseph James

Riding along on the horse and cart

We used to go hop picking at Champneys in Eridge, Sussex. Hop fields were all round the farms at Tonbridge Wells, Kippings Cross, Lamberhurst – all the way through. My children used to hate picking but when the time came for the men to collect the empty bines at the end of the day they enjoyed riding back to the farm on a horse and cart, sitting on top of the bushel baskets. That was the highlight of their day. It was lovely in sunny weather, but not so good when it was raining, with the mud. Of course your memory forgets the wet days. We used to be collected in the lorry and take us back at the end of the day.

Babs Woods

Some holiday!

Between '39 and '49, we were on a farm near Collier Street, Marden and saw Spitfires and Messerschmitts fighting overhead. And this other boy and I – we were only ten – were missing as usual from the huts and suddenly there were planes fighting each other and tracer bullets were flying right past us. They weren't going for us but as they were fighting above our heads we were caught in their line of fire. Anyway all my aunts and my mother were screaming. Mum was pulling her hair out, and I wouldn't go back, would I? I was just heading for the fields and stayed there until it was over. Eventually we all got back and this happened all the time, bombers coming over dropping bombs on us. They weren't bombing us in particular, but they had fighters going after them all the time all night so wanted to get rid of their bombs in case they were hit. Anyway the next day we were up and out, all of us.

George Bennett

A handy cleaner

Picking hops stained your hands all brown and it wouldn't come off with soap and water, but if you weed in a pot and washed your hands in it that brought them up clean. We learned that when we were picking at Tanyard Farm near Cranbrook. They had 120 hop huts there. We came down from Dagenham in Essex to hop-pick and while we were there I went to the local school in Cranbrook. All the adults used to go down to the pub at night and it was always noisy coming home because they sang as they walked along the lanes while one of the men played an accordion. When we were helping with the picking it was all 'What would you like to have with the money? Anything you like, a bike

maybe, or a doll's pram?' but when it came down to it and the Hoppers were paid off it was always the same – back to school with a new pair of shoes.

Ron Leonard

Pearly's hut is last of the line

We went back to visit our hop farm at Eridge a while ago and of all the hop huts that had stood in the row, ours was the only one left standing.

Nancy Arrowsmith, Pearly Queen of Whitechapel

Pearly Hoppers at Eridge

We picked our hops at Eridge. When we went back to look at the old place recently we took my mother and old Bert to the pub at Old Tudeley where we used to go after hopping in the evenings.

Margaret and Brian Hemsley,
Pearly King and Pearly Queen

Tom Johnson, Pearly King of Bow Bells and an ex-Hopper, with a London Bobby.

Margaret and Brian Hemsley with the author at Bodiam Hop Festival. (Story on p.58)

Pelletised hops

Hops are dried by the same process as instant coffee is made. The resulting pellets, known as hoplets, will keep well for three to four years when vacuum packed and put into cold storage. Each pack weighs a kilogram, or 2.205 lbs.

Mark Dobler

Dodging the bullets

We were picking at Guinness's farms at Bodiam before the war and we were here at Bodiam when war was declared on the 3 September. I remember German planes shooting at us in the fields as we worked. Guinness put all ditches around the fields so we had somewhere to go to escape the bullets.

F.W. Pooke

A wee gas attack

My mother had eight kids and my Aunt had ten. I was the second oldest at ten. We all had to wee in a bucket and washed the wee all over us because it was all on the news about gas attacks. I'd never heard of it before – never even heard mention anywhere before, but whether it's acid or something I don't know. Whether it would do any good at all I don't know but at least we all smelt the same. It wasn't terrible for us – we loved it as kids. It was just one big adventure!

George Bennett

See you later, Dad!

Grandfather Asquith didn't like the family going hop picking so when the long-awaited letter arrived from the farmer telling us he wanted our family for September, Grandma always hid it. When our Grandad came home one night after work he'd find that she and the kids had gone off hopping and he wouldn't see her for a month.

Tricia Walker (née Latham)

Labour Exchange found jobs for hop pickers

I was out of work in 1931 and went to the Labour Exchange (the first Job Centres) to see if they had anything for me. They gave me a travel voucher and the name of a farm where they needed pickers. I caught the train to Headcorn from Hoxton and was collected on a horse and cart. This was a very slow way to travel. Nowadays it would take forty-five minutes by car. It took us two-and-a-half hours to get to Goldwell Farm which was three-quarters of a mile along a farm track after the main road. The nearest village was three miles away. There were shops and pubs at Biddenden but it was quite a walk for your evening pint. Beer was a bit stronger in those days so quite a few of us landed in the ditches for the night. While we were picking we lived in Hoxton. The letter from the hop farm arrived in late August telling us they wanted us to go picking again. My brother made an oven out of a metal box so we could light a fire underneath to roast our meals. At one time the London blitz was so bad that Dad wrote to the farmer and asked if we could go there to work on the land, just to get away from all the bombs. But then the doodlebugs started and they were even worse so we ended up coming home again. As much as anything it was the excitement of the outing we liked. We hardly knew what grass was in Hoxton and there were all these lovely fields and countryside at Headcorn.

Reg Evans

Bin there, done that!

The bins into which the hops were picked were made of hessian fixed to a wooden frame, which consisted of two sets of wooden poles approximately six feet long. These were crossed and bolted together about a foot from the top in a V shape which allowed them to open and shut in a scissor-like movement and onto which the side poles carrying the hessian trough were fixed. There were also two pieces of wood some eight feet long, mortised into the uprights and protruding one foot at each end to form the handles with which to move the bin along the alleys between hop hills (or plants) as the bines were cleared and the bin needed to be lifted nearer the fresh bines. Some of the bins were divided with a piece of hessian sewn across the middle to make two half bins for people who were picking on their own. The V at the top of each of the bins originated from the days when hops were only grown on poles before being superseded by wire work and hop string. The poles, complete with hop bines, were placed across the two V ends to facilitate picking. A man, the pole puller, was employed full time to pull the bines from the ground and place them across the bins.

Roger Jeffries

A quick way to make a new pond

On Godstone Hop Farm there is a large pond and it was created when a bomb dropped there by a Luftwaffe aircraft on its way back to Germany. The bomb crater later filled with water and has been a pond ever since.

Sharman Mayhew

Mind games

We were always playing games when we were down on the hop farm. While our parents were picking we'd say such things as 'think of a number, one to ten. Double it. Add five. Halve it. Take away the number you first thought of. The answer is two and a half' – or if you got them to add six the answer would be three because it was always half the number you gave them to add.

Bob Hill

The kindly gypsies

All our family went hopping every year. When it was time to go down to the hop gardens a lorry picked us up in Islington. I went to Boston Manor Farm, Yalding, to pick but stopped going when I was fifteen. I was one of the first to work on the machines when they came in, sorting out the leaves. Our sister was ill once with rheumatic fever and the gipsies camped near the farm looked after her while the rest of the family went picking.

Liz and Sylv Parkin

Country living

We stowed our faggots up against the wall of the hopping hut. When we went to collect them my brother and I went off round the farmyard to find two poles – there were plenty of them about – and we'd lay them parallel on the ground, then put several bundles of faggots across them so they were balanced. They were really heavy and we had to carry them across the field and up a hill back to the Clover Field. For two lads they took some shifting. Water was another problem as there was only one stand pipe in Clover Field so all the water we used had to be carried in buckets up the hill from the stand pipe and back to the huts. At the bottom of the hill was what looked like a little Indian village of huts. This was where we were; the huts for Mum, Gran, Nell, Pat, Ray Tony, Maureen and me. The toilet was near the standpipe and was like a long box with an equally long wooden seat with lots of holes in it for everyone to use. Underneath and just behind it was a trench and this was filled with lime every so often to disinfect the trench contents. Our beds were made from straw laid across faggots and covered with a sheet. It poked through the sheet and was killing to sleep on.

Terry Blackman

7 Home Dwellers

Bough Beech hop farm, now Kent Wildlife Trust nature reserve, has a small oast hop museum run by Ray Coles and Joan Medill. One year the reservoir overflowed; a mallard and ten ducklings were seen swimming across the car park. (Courtesy of John H. Clark)

For home dwellers the rewards were not always so great. Family members of hop farmers were expected to help as a matter of course and some jobs, such as twiddling new bines up strings, entailed long, tedious hours of work. Despite this, villagers were often glad of the opportunity for extra work right on their doorstep and in them, local hop farmers gained a useful source of necessary help at their busiest time of the year. Hop harvests took anything from two to six weeks according to the size of the hop gardens and it was essential to harvest as soon as hops reached their peak. With the vagaries of English weather anything could happen in that period, be it drought, gales or heavy rain and, like any other growing crop, hops needed to be gathered dry. Some hop gardens, particularly the smaller ones, used exclusively home dwellers, or local people, to pick their hops. Sometimes they could catch a bus to near the field where they would be working but mainly the bus service was only once or twice a week so most walked to work in the mornings and home again at night. It may seem leisurely, idyllic work to a town dweller but there is always something to do on a farm, not just in September when hops are picked, but right through the year. Work starts again as soon as the hop harvest has been collected in. The plucked bines need to be burned or put down as matting by the farm gate

Bough Beech oast and wildfowl centre, Ide Hill.

for cattle coming up twice a day to be milked, or by water troughs where the mud is often hock deep. Broken strings need to be replaced, poles inspected for cracks and wires for tautness. New stock plants needed planting out in September or October then banking up with earth. Hopping implements require checking for wear, particularly scuppets, which may need their sacking trays replaced. Previously, when farmers used stilt walkers to string the overhead wires, the ten or twelve-foot wooden stilts required overhauling to ensure they were safe to use. Crops need spraying with fungicide against blight and insecticide against aphids and other attacking insects. A constant watch for signs of blight is essential as, once established, it sweeps across hop gardens like wildfire, killing off thousands of bines.

Bough Beech

Near Ide Hill, Kent, is an early nineteenth-century oast known as Bough Beech. Although the property is now owned by the water board, the Kent Wildlife Trust manages the building, carefully retaining its character as a working oast with its major features still in situ. If such names as hop dog, scuppet, hop press, nidget and bine hook rouse happy memories, they can all be seen at Bough Beech. There is an unusual humidity meter, once kept in the holds of sailing ships when hops were shipped to Australia in the good old days. The nature reserve around the oast house has a wealth of Kentish flora and fauna, particularly birds. Anyone wishing to view inside the oast, see how hops were dried, and how they are still grown is welcome to visit Bough Beech's working hop garden (telephone number 01622 662012) from April to October.

Roy Coles and Joan Medill

Time to go hopping

We didn't get a letter from the farmer inviting us to pick – we just went, year after year, knowing we were needed. It went round by word of mouth. Someone would say 'They're picking up, starting next Monday', so you'd go down ready to meet the lorry. It was probably the Londoners who got letters, not us. They didn't have Londoners at our farms. They were all local. The lorries took them back to their own homes after the day's picking. It annoyed us when the measurers came round with their bushel baskets if they pressed down hard on the hops and we'd have a go at them and they'd tip them all out and come back for more; sometimes they'd press them down hard as well. It was a London lady that taught me how to do the hops. She was the first from London we'd ever seen. She'd say 'It's too clean' and she'd throw leaves in and bits of twigs. We weren't dirty pickers because we went to the same farms every year, but she showed me how to do it quicker than we were doing.

Babs Woods

Sally Natcutt's family, The Taylors, with two friends at Days Farm, Hunton nr Yalding.

Grudge fights

They used to come from Brighton to Brede to pick at our farm in Stubb Lane, and you'd hear lots of stories in the village about the fights between the locals and the London Hoppers who were not always popular. I can remember we were allowed extra rations for the cheese for our sandwiches during the war, and it was always in order that we had a new school uniform and new clothes from the money we earned – that was always after hop picking. It was all Guinness's down in our area.

Peter Maylem

Glow worms and haloes

We'd taken six chickens down with us on the train, all live in a sack, and on one journey they all got out and they were messing all over the seats. Fortunately the windows were closed. We got to Paddock Wood station where they used to stop before Beeching closed all the branch lines – we had to change at Paddock Wood to go on to Cranbrook – and once there threw all our

bundles out on the platform. You'd just grab your own bundle but one day my old Gran said someone had pinched her bundle so she pinched someone else's. And we got on the next train to Cranbrook and had about a three-mile walk from Cranbrook with all our 'opping pots and prams and all our bundles, and us children at the time (about 1949, 1950) we used to find glow worms glowing in the hedges and my Gran put them in our hair and it made us look as if we had halos as we walked along in the dark. The gipsies would hear us and see us coming and they put all pots on with water to make us hot cocoa when we got to the site. When we got there my dad went down to the faggot stack to get the faggots for making the bed and straw to fill the mattress. My Grannie Tilly was filmed years ago by the BBC when Eamonn Andrews did a documentary on her. They came down the hop garden of the farm we were staying on because my Gran at the time was the oldest hop picker of Great Britain. They filmed her. They brought in Randolph Sutton, an old singer, and he came and sang all the old hopping songs for her. We kids used to go out black-berrying and bring them back to my Mum and she would make a great big pie, one as big as a baby's head, and she'd boil it in the hopping pot while we all stood round singing a hopping song.

A lady visitor to the Kent and East Sussex Railway Hop Festival, 2003, who did not give her name.

Goods Hill Farm, Tenterden

I was brought up on a farm where we had hops, in Tenterden. My mother and father and grandparents lived there. We had the London Hoppers down for the hop picking but when it became difficult with more regulations about toilets and that we went over to local pickers. We were at Goods Hill Farm, up on the Cranbrook Road from Tenterden. I wrote my life story down for Age Concern recently because the hops were such a large part of my life. The Londoners had a whale of a time really. Our Hoppers didn't stay in Hopper huts. We had a huge grainery and my father arranged for it to be all emptied out and whitewashed and all that,

Delivery day at Larkins

and they used to have to lie on the floor. There were sections for washing and eating, and upstairs, it was huge upstairs, they curtained it all off for all the different families. They slept in the loft and lived downstairs. They had the cook house outside and my mother would get vexed with me because I was so fussy as a child: I wouldn't eat this and I wouldn't eat that. But when the Hoppers were there I used to go round and sit in the cookhouse and eat with them. 'You won't eat at home but you'll eat round with them' she'd say crossly. My father did the hop drying while my mother did the measuring.

Kathleen Balkham née Levitt

Born under a gooseberry bush

My sister Nelly, who was five years older than me, and I went hop picking every year with our mother, as did most of the families from Keatons Road in Bermondsey. Dad was a lighterman so could only come down at the weekends as he had to work on the Thames barges the rest of the week. At one place we burned faggots in the fire and had to go and collect them by the bundle. I remember seeing a lady with a little baby and asking her how babies were born. She and the other women laughed when she said 'they are born under a gooseberry bush', so I knew it wasn't true.

Sidney Fagan MA

Spring jobs

Early in the year, before it was time to attend school, Mother and I went to work in the hop gardens. Her job was training the new hop tendrils, winding them round the strings from left to right, unlike runner beans which climb the other way. The men did hop stringing; strings ran up to an overhead wire fixed to the top of hop poles and the men would have hooked them up there at the start of the year, using a long pole with a hook on the end. These strings were pulled down together with the bine when it was picking time in August or September.

Adele Coles

A real hopping family

My mother and I did the picking. My father grew a hop called Golding, so we always started hop picking before anyone else because they were ready early, so we usually had the Press there every year, taking photographs to put in the papers. I've still got a lot of pictures of my father drying the hops.

Kathleen Balkham née Levitt

Hop tokens at Larkins. Stephen Langridge paid his hop pickers with these tokens. At the end of 'hopping' they would be exchanged for money. The tokens were cast with Stephen's initials and the number of bushels picked. Stephen Langridge died in 1857. (Courtesy of Iain Ross-McLeod)

The caring Sally Army

We worked on Bull Farm in Cranbrook which was owned by Mr Rogers. My Aunt, Mrs Elizabeth Norton, was a twiddler on Bull Farm for fifty years. The Cambridge University students came down to our farm, erected a huge marquee and entertained the Hoppers with singing and country dancing. Back in London they held a party for us as a reunion. During the hopping season a medical centre was run in a little hut by the Sally (Salvation) Army. When we went hopping when I was a small child of two or three we lived in a huge wooden house which we called 'Noah's Ark'. There was one hopping family to each room. It was on the farm so there was no extra travelling. One day I jumped off something I'd been climbing up and landed straight in the hopping pot and scalded my legs badly. It was the Sally Army who looked after me. When war broke out the authorities came down and we were evacuated from Bull Farm, complete with all our hopping gear to Staffordshire, outside Stoke on Trent.

Ellen Lanksford

Fancy dress Pearlies

We represent the Lewes Commercial Square Bonfire Society and have been dressing up as Pearlies for many years now. We always go to the hop festivals whenever they are on.

Marion and Bill Weeding

Bell Common

My grandfather, John Grimes, came to live in Paddock Wood in 1880 and was in charge of the women workers and hop pickers. One of his jobs was to arrange for rows of bell tents to be put up in a field before the Hoppers were due to arrive. This is where the families lived while they were picking in the gardens. All the tents had to be fully inspected before dismantling after the hopping was finished and if a family had infected them with fleas or lice that tent had to be burned. One woman and her children came down in the night and needed a hut. She only had a shilling and a halfpenny. Despite it being dark and so late in the night, grandfather managed to find her a good hut and she wanted to give him something for his trouble so, although she couldn't see what she was doing in the dark, she plunged her hand into her pocket intending to give him the halfpenny which was much the same size as the shilling. It wasn't until later she found she had accidentally given him the shilling which was all the money she had for feeding herself and her children for the first week of hop picking!

Rhoda and John Grimes

All the fun of childhood

We would have liked to have had my dad, George, down picking with us all the time but he had to keep on at his job in Tonbridge Wells. Most years, hop picking went on for about four or five weeks and to me those times were the happiest memories of a very happy childhood. This was because, although we did have to pick on a pretty regular basis, Mum used to let us have our playtime in the fields. Of course after our evening meal we were allowed to play outside the huts until it got dark. Usually after that we were too tired to do anything but settle down for a good night's sleep, and mighty tired we were. The next day it started all over again, up early and off to pick in the fields.

Patrick Conner

Lethal insects

Mostly I remember the smell of wood smoke from our campfires. It was lovely. What I didn't like were all the insects, particularly the crane flies, which we knew as daddy long legs. They got caught up in your hair and were hard to get out again. We children were really scared of the dragonflies that hovered around the pond – we had been warned that if they bit you, you dropped dead on the spot, so for a long time we thought of them as lethal despite their attractive iridescent blue-green colouring. I was often glad to get back to London to escape from them. What I really loved was the smell of the hops; a bitter aroma.

Sidney Fagan MA

Happy times to remember

From 1910 to 1925 there were hop gardens wherever you looked in the Guestling area. My mum was a hop picker and is now ninety-six years of age. She has been living in the same cottage in Chapel Lane for over seventy years.

Maurice Sargent

Nearly a century ago

It seems a long time ago, now that I am ninety-eight years old and my daughter is seventy-five but when she was three years of age I used to take her hop picking and she would stand beside me at the bin as I pulled the hops off the bine. My hands got all black with the hops' juice and when you went to eat your lunch everything you touched tasted bitter from the hops.

Mary Abell (neé Laycock)

Skinner's coaches

Although the farm we worked on mostly took local pickers and occasionally some from as far away as Hastings, there were others, small farms,

Maurice Sargent with his friends, Bobby and Ivy Thomas, September 1953.

in the area that just took day pickers. These were Hastings families, usually transported every day in smart dark blue coaches owned by Skinners. Sometimes they came by truck. There were lots of smaller farms in the surrounding country areas: Udimore, Westfield Brede, Northiam and other nearby villages but I have no personal recollections of the people or where they went, only what I was told at the time and over the years. After picking was over, which usually lasted for two or three weeks, it was back home and off school for the new term for us. I started work in 1950 and did not go hop picking again after that.

Alfred H. Robinson

Merricks Farm

We went hop picking at Merricks Farm at Snailham and Doleham near Icklesham. That was back in 1944 until 1947. The whole family went every day. We travelled in the back of a truck from Hastings. I was seven years old when we started and the last time we went I was ten years of age. My father was a fisherman but he was injured in the war so had to be what they called a 'man at home'. We were very poor and money was hard to come by, so I had to walk down to the boat at Hastings every day and carry the fish home to be cleaned and Mum had it everywhere – fish in the sink, fish in the bath, buckets and anything else that would hold it.

Peter Veness

A pickers' party

We went hop picking at Hartlip on Wakeley's Farm. We had to be up at 5.00 a.m. ready to jump on the back of a lorry which drove us out to the hop fields. When we pulled the early morning bines we'd get drowned because they were covered in dew. At the end of the hopping season, Wakeley's always organised a party evening for the pickers.

Ian Bennett

Guinness's pickers

My first recollections of hop picking are from about 1940, when I was six. Our family always picked at Guinness's, New House Farm, Bodiam. This farm only took pickers from the surrounding villages and Hastings. Some of those travelling up from Hastings stayed in huts on the farm to save them the long journey back and forth each day. The huts were situated in a long line at the side of a field and were surrounded by hop gardens on three sides with a field in front. It was about a quarter of a mile from the village. There were approximately thirty huts and one old caravan. The same families came down year after year. Some of them I can still remember: starting from the hut at the bottom there was Mrs Blackman (or Blackford); then the Latters (John, known as Podge, Sheila, Ruby, their Mum and Dad.) Next were the Coopers – I can only remember Freddie. The Woods were next; Jimmy and Dennis. These first five or six huts were made of timber and larger than the remainder which were constructed from corrugated iron sheets. Next was a covered area for drying clothes and, I assume for cooking purposes when it was raining. The next hut was occupied by my Auntie Ada Barrow and cousins, Terry, Jeannie and David. Their father, my uncle, was a pig breeder and came over to help pick when work allowed. Next came some families whose names escape me but other members of

our family were at about hut fifteen – my Auntie Ada Morrell and her husband, Alf, as well as my cousins Johnnie, Sheila and Vicky. We were in the next hut, number eighteen. After that there was the old caravan that housed Tom and Mrs Bird and their daughter Hester. Back in the corrugated huts was another of my aunties – Auntie Lily with cousins Shirley and Jimmy Beeching. There were a number of other huts, up to number thirty I believe, but I cannot recollect any one else's name. The whole family were pictured on the front of a Readers' Digest book *Yesterday's Britain*, with my Dad in the background and some of the Latter family as well. The picture was taken in about 1951.

Alfred H. Robinson

For a few pennies

We lived near the Guinness hop gardens as children and went hop picking just to earn a few pennies' pocket money. I remember pulling down the bines as a kid and pulling the hops off and putting them in the baskets.

David Colman

Dad was away in the army during the war

My father was not with us during the early part of the war as he was up in Scotland and the Shetland Isles, serving in the Army. Similarly Uncle Jim Beeching was in the Army in Burma. Cooking the evening meal back at the huts was done over open fires and it was us kids who collected the wood faggots from the huge pile at the top of the field. Picking usually started at 7.30 a.m., and finished about 4.00-4.30 p.m. We had a midday break and at this time usually ate sandwiches with a drink of cold tea or hot tea made in a billy can over a little camp fire. It had a lovely smoky taste and I still like it occasionally today. As kids we had to pick our quota of hops every day into a variety of containers as the bins were too high for us to reach comfortably. So we used buckets, up-turned umbrellas, old five-gallon oil drums or whatever came to hand. As soon as we had picked our quota we could go off and play, usually scrumping apples or climbing trees. There were also wild damson plums and hazel nuts to collect.

Arthur H. Robinson

'Pull no more bines'

We went to Halls Farm in Marden, Kent. We left home very early and walked to London Bridge station with Mum, my three brothers and myself, along with the hopping cart with all we needed for our five weeks' stay. We were met at Marden station by Bert with his horse and wagon. He took all the hopping carts to the farm while we walked. We lived in corrugated-iron huts with no windows but our Mum made the hut nice. When it rained it was very noisy on the tin roof. The farmer left bundles of straw to fill our mattress and pillows. The whole family slept top to bottom, but when my brothers got older, Mum got another hut for them. We got up very early to go to the hop field and stayed there all day until 'Pull no more bines!' was called. We ate lunch there – usually cheese sandwiches – Mum had a primus stove for boiling the kettle for making tea.

Joan Lewer née Thirkell

The hop gardens of Guestling Thorn

People came from out of the nearby towns on the buses provided and from London on trains and lorries. Some slept in huts on the farm. Many pickers took their two weeks holiday at this time so they could earn extra money to buy clothes for their children before they returned to school as money was hard to get. My mum worked for many years in the hop gardens. Her maiden name was Ethel Jury at the time she lived on Pound Farm at Guestling. Her parents, my grandparents, were the farmers there in the early 1900s. She also did hop picking for the Witherdens who then owned Copshall Farm at Guestling Thorn. The hop gardens were in Butchers Lane. Later in the year, after the hops were picked, these gardens were used for growing cabbages and other vegetables. The hops were

brought to Pound Farm for processing in the oast house there but this has now been turned into living accommodation having been converted.

Maurice Sargent

A bit of a flirt

My mother insisted that we helped her to pick for at least half an hour before we were allowed to go off exploring. I remember one year, Dad's sister-in-law, who was a bit of a flirt, was chatting up the good-looking poler who pulled down the bines for us. The others teased her unmercifully and called out 'Hey, Kate, it looks like you've clicked!'

Sidney Fagan MA

New House Farm, Bodiam

My family picked at New House Farm, Bodiam from 1940 until the 1950s, all through the war years. When the German bombers came over we all had to run to the ditch while the air raid was on. Our air-raid warden was Mrs Blackman and she was very deaf so instead of warning us, she was always the last person to hear the sirens going. We were all already in the ditches by the time she said anything! We stayed in huts on the farm but they were mainly locals who picked at New House. We came up from Hastings for about three weeks at a time.

Alf Robinson

Picking at sixpence a time

I used to get sixpence a bushel when I picked, just up the road from Bodiam station. I also picked at Bennet and Willis's Farm at Horsemonden and my wife picked at Hawkurst. My brother used to go out picking at Bodiam when he was a lad at London University.

Freddie Ganny

A family history among the hops

Several generations of our family worked with hops. My grandfather, uncle and father all dried hops on farms in the Paddock Wood area. Their

The old racking system at Harvey's Brewery, Lewes, Sussex.

wives and children were all involved throughout the year. My father, who was also a tractor driver, would dress the hops with various chemical washes during the growing season, probably spraying against the beautiful 'Hop Dog' caterpillar which we were always delighted to find when picking. They were really the caterpillar of the Tussack moth. They had hairs all over them in bright colours and a tiny tail which stood straight up in the air. It seemed quite a coincidence that the tractor, which was my father's pride and joy and was bright yellow, was also called a Caterpillar. Once, at the age of seven, I was allowed to help drive it through the hop fields.

Adele Coles

The good and the bad things about hopping

Hop picking had its down side occasionally. It was no fun picking hops with the rain running down the back of your neck right to your boots, and bines cutting into your hands, the odd wasp sting as well as some very annoying insects. But there are happy memories too, and these will be always in my mind: of the kettle boiling over the open fire, eating our grub lying on top of the old bines, the smell of the hops, the warmth of the sun, crisp September mornings, cries of 'hops ready!' at the start of the day and 'pull no more bines!' at the finish, of children laughing and crying and of happy Hoppers singing and joking. Memories like that will live with me all my days. Quite simply, I loved it.

Patrick Connor

8 Harvey's Brewery

Harvey & Son, Bridge Wharf Brewery, Lewes, East Sussex, founded by John Harvey, was under his management from 1783 to 1862. The first French Revolution was over by 1789 and a year later the brewery recorded supplying Old Red Port, sherry and claret to Lewes and surrounding villages. Without the benefits of electrical temperature controls, eighteenth-century brewing was prone to problems not met in modern processing. John Harvey records 'Warm day for brewing, worts cool badly. Second come down half past eleven in heat 66°' during the summer months, but in January he was noting the air was 'cool and frosty' and he found it necessary to 'put a fire round the tun (vat) to bring it on in heat'. The weather played an important part in brewing; too much rain affected the August barley and wheat crops which in turn could spoil the malts. He took a keen interest in experimenting with changes to the brewing processes. The brewery has its own supply of spring water from the nearby hills but at times river water had to be substituted when something went wrong, such as the pipes breaking.

In 1838 Harvey purchased the Bridge Wharf for £3,707. The site comprised three dwellings, two enclosed coal yards, a timber yard and two corn warehouses and benefited the brewery premises by connecting it to the nearby River Ouse. John built the Bridge Wharf Brewery on site, where the ground floor held bell-shaped oak vats brewing fifteen to twenty barrels per day. A four-horsepower horizontal steam engine provided the necessary power and can still be seen in full working order on the premises.

Mr Anthony Jenner is the present Chairman and Joint Managing Director of this independent family brewery and Mr Miles Jenner has been

Harvey's Bridge Wharf Brewery, Lewes, Sussex, as it was a hundred years ago.

the head brewer since 1986. The brewery has been owned by the same family for seven generations of the Harvey family. The following information was supplied by Miles Jenner. For a family brewery to survive in the present climate it is essential that they have guaranteed outlets for their products and as a result, Harvey's now own thirty-three tied houses extending from Lewes as far as Maidstone and Midhurst.

Local hops

Sussex breweries tended to buy hops within a sixty mile radius of the brewery as this meant that farms and farmers were easily accessible for

The Alfred Shaw vertical steam engine at Harvey's brewery. This machine, together with the Pontifex & Wood flatbed steam engine, once drove all the brewery's machinery.

business and the breweries got to know the individual flavours of local hops. Some farms, such as Hollambies, have grown hops since Jacobean times.

East Kent Goldings, Fuggles, Progress, Bramley Cross and Sussex Goldings are the hop varieties most used by Harvey's. These are drawn from Wadbush, Robertsbridge, Cranbrook and the Wealdon areas.

Seasonal beers

Harvey's were the first brewery to conceive a special type of beer for different months of the year and although they brew Best Bitter, Blue Label and India Pale Ales (or IPA), Armada (a strongly hopped and tasting pale ale), Dark Mild and many types of beer all year round, other varieties come in at their own season.

'Kiss' is brewed in February and is named after Rodin's famous statue, 'The Kiss', which originally belonged to Lewes. Porter is made in March from a Victorian recipe of 1859. In May 'The Knots of May' is brewed and named after a local Morris side. 'Wheat Beer' is produced in June from copper wheat. The special brewing

Harvey's Brewery from the river at Lewes. (Courtesy of Iain Ross-McLeod)

for July Independence Day is a premium beer in memory of 'Tom Pain', a radical excise officer known as a stickler for duty. September sees the emergence of 'Southdown Harvest' ale. From 1 October until 1 of the following May is 'Old Ale', similar to pre-war mild ales. November calls for 'Bonfire Boy' and December to January has its 'Christmas Ale' which has an alcoholic volume of 8.1%. 'Nuts Brown Ale' is so called historically because of the roasted malt and caramel sugars which produce a nutty flavour. Occasionally Harvey's create a new beer in commemoration of a particular date or event.

Low alcohol beers

In 1988 Harvey's launched their new low alcohol beers onto the market.

Low alcohol does not mean short on flavour and in keeping with today's determination to cut down on drinking and driving and in association with CAMRA (The Campaign for Real Ale, Ltd) Harvey's produce two low alcohol beers, 'John Hop' and 'Bill Brewer'. The Long Man Morris side of Morris dancers have created a handkerchief dance in tribute to 'John Hop'.

How beer is made

Beer is a fermented liquor made by using yeast and barley, which manufactures malt. Yeast is a living, micro-cell organism which feeds on the sugars and converts them into alcohol. The process is known as fermentation. During the production of beer the sugars from barley are used to produce fermentation. Barley, with its long 'ears', is the earliest known cereal cultivated by Man. A grain of barley consists of a seed embryo together with a store of insoluble starch and protein wrapped in a cellulose cell. Some barleys germinate faster than others so barley type selection is important to produce a good beer. Moisture helps dissolve the cellulose and encourage the seed to germinate. This is the basis of malt; the first step towards producing beer.

Top: *Skimming the wort at Harvey's Brewery. (Courtesy of Iain Ross-McLeod)*

Middle: *Casks waiting to be racked at Harvey's Brewery. (Courtesy of Iain Ross-McLeod)*

Bottom: *Nineteenth-century flat bed steam engine at Harvey's Brewery. (Courtesy of Iain Ross-McLeod)*

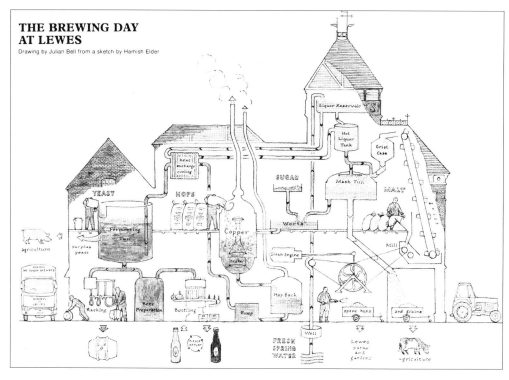

THE BREWING DAY AT LEWES

Drawing by Julian Bell from a sketch by Hamish Elder

The full procedure at Harvey's brewery for producing the beer.

Using the barley

Barley is steeped in water, the quality of which is essential as it beneficially or adversely affects the flavour of the beer, as water steeped in peat affects the flavour of whisky. Malt gives beer the major part of its taste, colour and body. In a brewery, water is referred to as liquor. The barley absorbs moisture and oxygen and when ready, is spread out on a malting floor where for five days it is warmed, turned and kept at an even temperature before germination until the maltster assesses the correct time for Kilning, or drying the grain with a gentle flow of hot air. Any rootlets produced during this stage are filtered out and sold as chicken feed while the best grains are sent to the brewery where it is crushed in a mill. This flattens the husks allowing the grain to spill out. The mixture of whole husks and grain is known as grist and is transferred to the grist case.

The importance of pure liquor in brewing

Harvey's use fresh spring liquor pumped directly to an overhead reservoir fitted immediately above the mash tun, then filtered down through a hot liquor tank and boiled to a sustained temperature of 158° F. Grist and hot liquor are fed simultaneously into the mashing machine and mixed, producing mash which drops into the mash tun at 150°F. This produces wort and the process takes just forty-five minutes when it is allowed to stand. The worts are filtered through a wort safe where they are checked to ensure they are 'bright'. They are then collected in a copper where flavouring hops are added and the brew is boiled for one-and-a-half hours. As the wort is run off, rotating sparging arms sprinkle liquor across the surface of the mash to flush out the remaining malt sugars. The spent maltings or grains are high in protein and once the process is completed they are sold off for nutritious feed to dairy farmers and racehorse trainers, and help to keep the animals in top performance. Some beers are conditioned in casks while others are conditioned in the brewery where it is filtered and kegged, giving it a longer storage life.

The function of hops

It may come as a surprise to hop pickers, but ale can be produced without the addition of hops. According to ancient record it was either the Romans or invaders from Belgium or Germany who introduced the hop to Britain. They largely fell out of favour when Henry VIII decided he preferred his ale without the taste of hops, and it wasn't until after his death that they again came into preference. Since then they have been an essential ingredient of Man's favourite brew. The secret lies at the base of each petal where a small seed forms an integral part of hop cones or flowers. It is the resins and oils at the heart of this tiny seed, about the size of a grain of mustard seed, which not only provides the well-known bitter flavour of beers, but also a natural protection against micro-organisms which could spoil the beer.

Transporting the finished product

Harvey's was established long before the advent of railways, lorries and high speed transport. It was usual for a brewery to delivery their wares to hostelries and inns within a twenty-mile radius of the brewery and horse drawn drays and manual transportation using handcarts were the order of the day. It was because of the ease of mobilizing their wares further afield that Harvey's bought the river site it now occupies and employed barges to ferry their beer along the River Ouse. Nevertheless as new inventions revolutionised the transport industry Harvey's kept up with the times as beer is a perishable product and needs to reach its market as early as possible. Once a cask or keg is opened it will not stay saleable for longer than five days. In 1906 Harvey's took advantage of the new steam powered vehicles and bought a Bauly wooden wheeled, solid rubber-tyred 'overtype' Foden

Malt store at Harvey's. Unusually, these old barrows have wooden wheels.

steam wagon supplied in the Scammell's livery. The model was not supplied with a trailer so a once horse-drawn dray was brought into service and fixed at the back to enable the vehicle to pull a full load of casks. Legally, it was only allowed to travel at a top speed of 8mph. By the 1920s the Bauly was replaced by a Foden overtype steam dray based on the popular and powerful traction engine. This was a great advancement as it was capable of hauling a six-ton load with a further four tons on a rear trailer and was allowed to travel at 10mph. To keep it powered up it required about half a hundredweight of coal for every ten miles travelled. By 1934 Harvey's were using diesel-powered lorries with pneumatic tyres and increased speeds up to 20mph. This

Copper mash tun at Harvey's Brewery. (Courtesy of Iain Ross-McLeod)

miracle of transportation did fourteen miles to the gallon when hauling six tons of barrels on its dray plus a further six on a trailer. When hauling a mere six tons and without the trailer it made eighteen to twenty miles-per-gallon.

Brewery horses

During the horse-drawn dray days of plying trade Harvey's recorded horses in their stable with names such as Duke, Boxer, Damsel, Trotter, Violet, Bob and Rodney. Old Georgey was a well-remembered and loved bay cob which pulled Harvey's brewery drays for over thirteen years and is commemorated by a silver inkwell set in a horse's hoof with 'In memory of

Old Georgey 1876' inscribed on the lid. The stables can still be seen at the end of the brewery yard. One night a disaster struck the stables. A railway embankment collapsed upstream near Barcombe Mills, causing the river to flood without warning. The high volume of water cascaded downstream at a forced pace, sweeping over the banks, level with and across Harvey's yard into the stables. Henry Barrett's son, a carter, recalled being woken by the sound of threshing hooves and the snorting of terrified horses down in the stables. He rushed downstairs and waded across the yard to the rescue. The horses were wild-eyed with fright and he had trouble unfastening their halter ropes before leading them to the safety of higher ground.

9 Happy Memories

Mrs Jill Poile and family: Sid, Nora, Maud, Joan and Mum. Pre-war.

How precious and individual are our reminiscences. An anecdote shared is even more treasured. It is our memories that make us unique: we are the sum of our yesteryears. I have frequently found that, while two people may have taken part in the same event, their accounts may differ on several points. However, while, on the whole, hop pickers seem less prone to varying the story, I have had some readers come to me and say 'it wasn't like that at all'. That may be so. But the way these reminiscences are told is from our own yesterdays and we should accept that Hoppers' tales are how those particular people remember them and that is how they are

recorded. With this in mind, enjoy the uniqueness of these told tales and the individuality of the people who tell them. It is important to record these potted histories. Where once families sat round the dinner table or fireplace in the evenings and recounted their day, regaled their children with family stories, events and generally passed on the family's history by word of mouth, this rarely happens now. In today's household the family may not even assemble around the table together for a meal and they are more likely to sit round the television than a warm fire. There are fewer opportunities to share the day's events and to weave the family's

Ben Tomsett's (in glasses) at Fowle Hall Farm, Paddock Wood at Crittenden Farm, Hatfield Hoppers' party celebrating end of 1956 hopping season. Lady holding a cup is Adele Cole's aunt, hop dryer's wife Violet Worsley. Bill Green, in pullover, and pickers.

historic web. A memory not recorded is a piece of history lost forever if no one is left to remember it. Hop picking and all it entailed was such a vibrant, colourful part of English life it would be sad if this mosaic of memories were to be lost forever, merely for the sake of writing it all down.

Bare knuckle fights

My Nan was born in Goudhurst in a farmhouse and remembered very well the days of hop picking. This was an area where the men used stilts to string the poles. When the hop season was on us, all the village folk were involved in the picking and the children were given upturned umbrellas to collect the hops in before one of the adults transferred them to the bushel baskets.

As well as the local people, the East Enders used to come down in carts laden with all the things they would need for the weeks they were there. The gypsies came as well with their brightly painted caravans. Each group kept themselves separate and had no contact with the others. There were often fights between the gipsies and the East Enders. The gipsies used bare knuckles as it would have been looked at as a disgrace to pull out a knife. Many of the shops put up shutters at this time as all Londoners were thought to be thieves. Goudhurst is one of the few places in Kent where there are still several hop fields. My Nan was so fond of those days of her youth that if any of us went into the hop field area during the picking season she asked us to gather a few hops from beside the hedgerow and take them home to her so she could test their quality.

Fran Price

'Pull no more bines!'

There were set times to start and finish each day. These were defined with shouts of 'all to work!', 'all to dinner!' and, at the end of the day, 'pull no more bines!'. This last call was usually heard about half an hour before the pickers went home or back to their huts and allowed them to finish picking the bine in hand and for the measurer to come round, measure up the hops and empty the bins. It was usually his job to see that the pickers had cleaned up any spilt hops left around the bins before they went home.

Roger Jeffries

Nicking sweets

While we were in the fields picking, a young man came most weeks with a tray of things for sale. He was a bit simple and the children took advantage. One day he was complaining to some of the mothers 'I've been told that a lot of the children have been stealing from me. They shouldn't do that you know.' While he was telling them this the children were busy nicking sweets from his tray as he was talking. Some of the women were unsympathetic and said it served him right if he was so simple he let them get away with it, but I was sorry for him as he was a friendly chap.

Sidney Fagan MA

Last night sing-song

My mum usually came down to the farm while dad worked in the docks. I was about four years old when we started and about twelve or thirteen when we last went which was in November 1981. I remember the good times; the chalet huts, scrumping, sitting in the warm oast house with all the other kids and singing together on the last night before going home. We had a right knees-up. Dad was a pole puller and Grandma loved to come down picking too, with all my aunts.

Maud Reynolds (née Tidy)

German prisoners helped with the rescue

We picked at Hertsfield Farm in Stylebridge. One year the farmer planted a whole field of American hops so this meant we pickers had to stay on until October because of the extra field to pick.

German prisoners of war were sent to the farm to work. There were three or four to a farm. One of the huts was known as Black Barn and one night it burnt down. It was the German prisoners who went into the flames and helped to get the children out.

Pat Bevan (née Valler)

Maxi's Taxis

When it was time to go down to the hop gardens several families got together and hired a lorry. It was known as 'Maxi's Taxis'. Everything that we

Bobby Foster, Maude Betts, Marion Barton, Mrs Busby, Jill Poile.

could possibly need was packed into tea chests, which were then loaded onto the back of the lorry while we all sat on top. It was scary on the lorry as we had to travel all the way from Dagenham in Essex right down to our farm in Kent. I hated it when we went through Blackwall Tunnel. It was really noisy and the white tiled walls were covered in soot and it all got in your hair. We picked hops all week and would then sub some money on the Saturday when Grandad came down. He and Mum would go down to the local pub at Marsden and by the time the evening was over they'd spent all the subs. They would stagger home across the unlit fields and many was the time they fell into one of the many ditches along the way!

Rose Etherington

Hard work for little reward

The pickers picked all day while the emptying and measuring was performed twice a day by the farmer, once around lunch time and again at the end of the day. He would take the hops out of the bin by scooping with a bushel basket and filling it within three or four inches of the top. If the pickers had worked hard sometimes as much as twenty or thirty bushels could be taken out of one bin according to how many pickers contributed to the picking. The tally would be recorded on the picker's card so the farmer knew how much to pay us later. Sometimes there were arguments between the farmer and a picker who would accuse the farmer of filling the bushel basket too full, or if there were too many leaves and bits of bine the farmer told the picker to take them out and he'd go back later to take their tally after he had measured everyone else's hops. I recall one incident with one of the London pickers who, while her hops were being measured, said 'You're taking those a bit 'eavy, guv.' 'They are fair' he replied, carrying on. After another couple of bushels were taken she was still not satisfied and said 'They're still 'eavy!' and with that, as he bent over the bin to scoop up the next bushel, the woman stuck out both her hands and pushed his head into the bin. Needless to say the farmer was furious and said

'I'm knocking two bushels off your tally for that!' With the price for picked hops set at six bushels for a shilling that was quite some penalty!

Roger Jeffries

Friendly rivalry

We picked on Pixel Farm at Hawkhurst. There were fifty huts for us pickers to live in while we were there. They had two kinds of huts, the corrugated ones and ones built of bricks; these were the best kind as they were warmer and dryer. If you and your family had been picking there as regulars for a few years you were given one of the brick huts.

Saturday night we went to the local pub and the Hoppers 'went to town'. We Londoners and the local Hoppers were friendly rivals and you'd hear them calling out to each other 'we picked a lot more than you today!'.

Ivy Dixon (née Smith)

The pangs of first love

When I was young I took a fancy to my cousin, Ivy, who was very pretty. We used to get on well and went off round the hop farm exploring together. Unfortunately one year another boy came down picking and she started going out with this other lad and ignoring me. I had always wanted her to like me and was jealous of him, but Ivy and I remained friends long after that.

Sidney Fagan MA

Drying the hops

Once the hops had been unloaded up at the oast house they were spread out evenly over a circular mat made from horse hair which was stretched across a slatted floor. This allowed the heat to permeate through the hops. This floor was situated just beneath the conical part of the roundel of the oast and the capacity was around 1,000-1,500 bushels at a time. The man responsible for all the work in the oast was called a hop dryer and while drying was in progress he spent all his time in the oast, even sleeping nearby so he could keep an eye on the temperature which had to be exact. At the same time he had to keep a watchful eye on the hops at all times, occasionally turning some of them over as the heat from the charcoal burning fire situated on the floor of the kiln was somewhat uneven. The dryer also heated bars of brimstone which were placed in the fire in a long handled pan. The sulphur not only killed any insects but also gave the hops a distinctive flavour which later added to the taste of the beer. The fumes and moisture rose up through the cowl at the top of the cone and we could smell the pungent, yellow-tinted smoke seen escaping all the while the hops were drying.

Roger Jeffries

Dad had to stay at work

We went hop picking in Kent in the 1930s. It was a time which the people of Deptford looked forward to, as it meant they had (their only chance of) a holiday. We'd be down in the hop fields from 7.00 a.m. 'til 4.00 p.m. We used to get paid per bushel of hops. At the time I'm talking about they were 4s a bushel which was put down in a ledger and you'd be paid at the end of the season – although you could have a sub twice a week to enable you to get your food and drink and living expenses for you and your family. The husbands never came because they couldn't afford to give up their regular job; in those days they were lucky to be in work at all. All the children used to enjoy it. It was a holiday. You worried the life out of your mother when the sweet man, that we called the 'Lolly Man', came round, calling out 'Lovely lollies!' which used to be about a penny or tuppence a bag of different sweets.

Horace Arthur Carr

Reconnaissance for scrumping

My dad always came down at the weekend and during the daytime walked around the area so he got to know what's what, especially in the orchards. By the time night came he knew where all the best fruit and vegetables were and when it was all quiet he'd go out and scrump the best in the orchard for the family to eat.

Tricia Walker (née Latham)

Tempting apples

By the evening Mum had made good dinner. We all tucked in having only had snacks during the day. That first evening Sally and I took the baby in the pram and went for a walk around the farm with a Bermondsey neighbour, Brigette, and saw the hop fields where we would be working for the next few weeks picking the hops from which we knew they'd make beer. We wandered down a lane past the farmer's house and thought how rich he must be to own all this! Just past the house was an apple orchard. There were no fences between the road and the fruit laden trees and there were all those rosy red apples lying on the ground. Brigette said it was all right to have them so Sally and I rushed across to collect as many apples as we could and put them on top of the pram. They were so juicy and sweet and we'd eaten quite a few before Mum warned us that we'd have stomach ache if we ate many more. The family budget in Bermondsey didn't allow for much in the way of fruit so it was a real treat to be able to munch apple after apple like that. The evening was chilly, a mist was coming in over the fields but the smell of the countryside was as delicious as the apples.

David Taylor

Marden Hoppers

Up until about thirty years ago Marden was a big hop growing area although, like the rest of Kent and Sussex, hop gardens have been in decline for the past fifty years. My house is called The Old Stocks and although it was built only eighteen years ago it stands on the original site of the village stocks which are now located in the churchyard at Marden. My house is one of eighteen built on the site of the old Hoppers' hospital which I can still remember seeing. Hoppers went there to have their injuries seen to when working in the hop fields. I first saw it in 1970 but it had not been used as a hospital for some time: part had been converted into bungalow accommodation and the small hall was used for village social functions. A picture of the old hospital is displayed in the local Medical Centre, labelled 'Hoppers' hospital and rest'.

Roger Jeffries

The Poile family, taken about 1939.

Aircraft crash

There was a large tree on the farm known as 'The Grey Lady' and when we saw it at night while walking back from the hop fields we knew we were nearly back at the huts.

There was a hill near the hop garden and one day a plane was shot down there. We all rushed over expecting it was a German who'd landed but it was one of our pilots so we carried him shoulder high back to the camp.

We children used open umbrellas for holding the hops we picked and if we tried to sneak off to play mum would yell at us 'Come back here immediately and pick these hops!'.

Ivy Dixon (née Smith)

Hopping children missed out on essential schooling

Sometimes our cousins, the tougher side of our docker family, came down hopping with us. One year one of the brothers upset his younger brother by calling him 'Dopey' and he sulked a long time after that; his feelings were really hurt.

I went to a good school in Bermondsey but always felt I should have gone to grammar school, which I'd hoped to do. But as hop pickers we were always still down in the country picking when the new school year started and it was then that new maths topics were introduced, right at the beginning of term, so I usually missed out on all the explanations and maths was always difficult for me. It wasn't until many years later when I went to university and became a teacher I caught up with all I had missed out on as a child.

Sidney Fagan MA

Jack and Jill

Our family went hop picking at a little farm at Three Oaks, Beckley. The farmer was Mr Bates. We lived in tin huts with beds made from faggots of wood with a mattress brought down with us from home and put on top. Mum had a hopping box which held all we needed including the old saucepans and a big iron pot. We only had an open fire outside to cook on. Water was collected from a spring in the nearby woods and you had to carry it in buckets for about half a mile.

Jill Poile (née Betts)

Strike for an extra shilling

My mum thought we needed more pay for our work and when the farmer refused she shouted 'That's it. Down tools!' and walked off the fields followed by the other Hoppers. They wanted an extra shilling per bushel. We were friends with the Titcheners who were coal merchants from Peckham and used their lorry to bring Hoppers down to the farm with their hopping boxes. I remember we had to tie feathers onto the bines. This was probably to keep the birds off the new hops.

Pat Bevan (née Valler)

From pokes to pockets

Once dried, the hops were raked out of the kiln into the long cooling room where the press was also located, on the first floor of the oast house. The thoroughly dried hops were then pressed tightly into a hop pocket, which was a strong hessian sack some eight feet long and about two-and-a-half feet in diameter when filled and fully pressed with dried hops. The pocket was suspended through a hole in the floor and secured with a sling fixed in place by steel rings during the pressing process. When the filling was completed the top of the pocket was sewn with coping string to seal it. At this stage it weighed about one and a half hundredweight.

Roger Jeffries

Memories of faggots and straw

That first night we slept well in our bed of faggots and straw, warm as toast, all cuddling up together under the blankets. 'Snug as a bug in a rug' Mum used to say. Early the next morning we were woken to the sound of a bugle. It signalled the arrival of the baker's lorry at the farm to sell fresh bread and cakes. Mum took her

The Poile family hopping in 1935.

purse and rushed out to buy a loaf and some cakes, made a fire to boil the kettle and handed out tea all round. Tea in bed with a freshly baked cake was always the start of the day for us kids and we never thought that poor Mum had to get up an hour earlier than us to get the fire going and brew up the tea for us.

David Taylor

A young Hopper

I first went hopping at the age of seven months with my twin brother, Jack; yes, we were Jack and Jill. This was my father's idea to overcome arguments over what to call us when we were born. Mum must have had a hard job doing all the washing that two babies needed. Once we even came home from vacation in Slough to have a go at hopping. By the time we got home at the end of the season we'd have enough of the farmer's apples to last well into the new year. The photos are of my family and in-laws. They didn't used to dress up for such a mucky job. Your hands smelled for a long time after you came home, but it was a good time had by all.

Jill Poile (née Betts)

Tate & Lyle's special

We always looked forward to hopping. It was a four-week holiday. The only thing was, when it finished it meant we had to go back to school, and I was a one who didn't like school. I omitted to say how we got there. Well, some people used to go by train from New Cross station, which was a special train known as The Hoppers' Train. I can't quite remember the exact fare in the 1930s, but I remember the time when it was only two shillings return. My father working on the railway, never let us go on the hopping train but sent us on the ordinary passenger train, so we went in comfort. We used to have a cart, mostly consisting of a Tate & Lyle's wooden box because in those days Tate & Lyle used to deliver their sugar in cartons inside these wooden chests and everybody used to go for one of them to make their cart for hopping. My mother had the same cart for years, and admittedly we had to

change wheels occasionally, but we always took a spare pair of pram wheels with us.

Horace Arthur Carr

A hopping song

I remember some of the songs we sang round the fire after our days' work. They all had lively tunes. We could sway and clap to this one:

> *Our luvverly hops,*
> *Our luvverly hops,*
> *When the measurer he came round,*
> *Pick 'em up, pick 'em up off the ground.*
> *When he starts to measure*
> *He don't know when to stop so*
> *I, I, jump in the bin*
> *And take the bleedin' lot.*

Jenny Farrant

Before picking began

At 8.00 a.m. all the Hoppers walked across to the middle of the field to await the farmer, who arrived by jeep. He would stand up on the bonnet, welcome us all to his farm then tell us all the rules as well as the penalties for misbehaviour. Scrumping, that is stealing apples from the orchard, was a dire offence and if anyone was caught the whole family could be sent home. Mind you he knew our love for apples so he sold them cheap together with ice cream if we walked up to his farmhouse. We children were all frightened of the farmer.

David Taylor

Comforts of home

In the evenings when you'd finished picking we'd go back to the hut, which was where we lived and slept when we were not working. Mother would cook the dinner consisting sometimes of a rabbit that'd been caught, or a chicken that'd been 'found' and we'd all have a good meal. Of an evening we'd have a sing-song round the fire, which was an open fire and where we did the cooking then. It was on an open place outside the hut. At 10.00 p.m. it would be

Julie, Jim and Paul Wilson hop picking with Aunt Beaney. (Courtesy Jackie Francesco)

time for bed, which consisted of a straw mattress and what bedding your parents had brought from home which, in the case of my mother, was all clean sheets and blankets so we didn't rough it like a lot of people did.

Horace Arthur Carr

Just off the Old Kent Road

My father, Horace Arthur Carr, was born in April 1910 and died in December 1994 only a couple of months after he recorded some of his hopping stories about the 1930s for my daughter's school project. He could remember hopping tales told to him from the 1920s and even back as far as the 1800s. It shows how healthy ex-Hoppers are because he was working in his allotment just the day before he died, so his sudden death came as quite a shock to the family. Fortunately I had visited him only a few days before.

Dad was born and bred in a small terrace house in Juniper Place off the old Kent Road at the New Cross end. I was born in February 1947 not far away and we moved to Abbey Wood Estate in 1961. Grandad, Dad's father, worked for the London, Brighton & South Coast Railway as a porter at the Old Kent Road station and then as a lamp foreman at London Bridge where the 4.00 a.m. Hoppers' Special left to take Hoppers down to Kent. I believe his lamp hut was at the end of the 'old' platform 22.

Derek Carr

10 Fond Farewells

Hop pickers at Harts Green Farm in the 1920s. (Courtesy of Mrs D. Isaac)

All good things come to an end, they tell us, and these hop picking stories are our fond farewell to a life we loved, knowing it will never happen again in our, or anyone else's lifetime. It is our way of letting go. The world has moved on; many Hoppers believe it is not necessarily the better for it. Friendships forged in the hop gardens are for life. Despite some friends losing touch, there are still many reunions among former Hoppers. However we can still visit hop gardens in Kent and Sussex and pick bines if you know where to look (see my *Voices from Kent Hop Gardens*). The camaraderie developed between Hoppers can only be matched by other close-knit communities sharing joys and hardships such as in the forces or among groups of people sharing intense, fraught situations. True camaraderie is harder to form these days where family bonds are less close. Making your own way while overcoming hardship builds character, self reliance and competency as any ex-Hopper will agree.

A special hopping box

The second year our family went hopping Grandad built a lovely hopping box on four wheels with a pram handle at one end. He painted it green. He also made a long bench on which five little bums could sit. Mum had a primus stove this time which boiled the kettle quickly, but she always managed to cook us filling meals on the camp fire.

In the mornings the bread man came to the garden and Mum bought us a cake, the likes of which I have never seen since. I usually left the field half an hour before Mum so I could get the kettle going for a nice cup of tea. As the years went on Mum got a brick hut and made it look nice by putting curtains up. We slept on wooden boards off the floor, which was lovely.

One evening when my brother John hung his jumper on a nail above the bed, a little field mouse unexpectedly fell out of his sleeve onto the bed. You never heard so much swearing in your life and there was a mass exodus from the hut until we were sure the mouse had gone!

Sally Nattcutt

Real friends

I really enjoyed working in the hop gardens, as did most pickers. There was always an atmosphere of camaraderie and enjoyment among everyone working there even though the Second World War was being fought at the time. Sadly, hop growing has declined dramatically over the last three decades and methods of picking and drying have changed. Now the bines are cut down from the back of a tractor and carted off directly to the oast building where they are picked by machine. The modern method is not so labour intensive as the old ways, and requires just a small number of people fetching hops from the garden while a few more work on the machine, picking out leaves. Powerful oil burners are used for drying these days and, because they generate much more heat than by the old coal method, the quantity of hops dried in each kiln is greater than in the days of charcoal fires. But whatever method is used, the smell of drying hops still fills me with nostalgia.

Roger Jeffries

That early morning bine

The first bine had to be pulled by 7.00 a.m. It was wet, horrid and the dew ran down the back of our necks and wet us through. The cake man came at 9.00 a.m. and we children all picked like mad so that the adults would be pleased with us and give us pennies to go off and buy cakes.

Rose Etherington

Cutting the bread

The food we ate in the 'bad old days' was a lot better for us than the over-preserved, salted and sugared stuff we feed children nowadays. I've never suffered from asthma, indigestion and the illnesses children have today; I'm sure it was all down to fresh air and my mum's cheese

sandwiches. I can sit at the end of my garden today, and if someone has a wood fire going and as the smell drifts up to me I can think back to Bodiam as clear as if it was yesterday.

Terry Blackman

Those cold mornings

We went to Tenterden to pick every year at Goods Hill Farm and I remember how cold it was when we pulled the first bines.

Kathleen Balkham née Levett

White's Farm at Beltring

The Carr family was very large with ten surviving children. All went hopping at some time in their lives. They favoured White's Farm at Beltring, later owned by Whitbread, now the Hop Farm Country Park. I took Dad and Mum (now nintey-one years old and still living in Abbey Wood) back to Beltring some years ago when Whitbread still ran it and our visit brought back many happy memories. Although Dad was a keen photographer his interest seems to have developed after his hopping days because, regretfully, we have no family photos of hopping. I never went hopping, but I remember our neighbours, the Chandlers and the Rolls families, going down each year.

Derek Carr

'When the measurer, he came round...'

After the farmer lectured us on all his rules the Hoppers moved off into the hop field and chose a bin; basically a large, strong sack, open down one side and fixed to wooden carrying handles at each end with wooden bars down the side that we could sit on while we picked. We were given a bine and had to pull the hops off it into the bin. Twice a day the measurer came round and measured out the hops we had picked using a special bushel basket, shouting out the number at each bushel measured. The tallyman who came with him wrote down the amount on our card and noted it in his book.

David Taylor

Shopping was delivered to the gardens

People think it's a new idea, having food delivered to your door, but the International Stores brought all kinds of tinned and fresh food, cheese and sausages to the hop fields to sell. It was as well as we needed groceries and the nearest shops for us were at Northiam; only a small village then and not much bigger now.

Terry Blackman

Anglers

As a child I didn't like picking hops. It was boring, made your hands black and was hard to wash off. I sat with my brother and sister, John and Tricia, making mud pies out of the lovely red soil or would wander over to watch the tractor going about the hop field loaded with freshly picked hops ready to be taken to the oast for drying. I walked to the river one day and saw a man fishing. I watched him pulling fish out of the water and was fascinated. I sat silently behind him, studied his rod, line float and hook and watched how he went about it. Then I went off and cut down a supple branch from a tree, borrowed some strong cotton and a pin from Mum, used a twig as a float, an acorn for a weight and fashioned the pin into a hook shape, tying it on the end of the cotton. With bread for bait I sat fishing near the man. He saw what I was doing, called me over and put a handful of maggots in my shirt pocket to start me off. I used these maggots as bait and they caught me a small but magnificent perch. The excitement I felt on hooking that fish equalled the excitement of my first speedway night. When I hauled the fish up onto the bank I hollered 'I've got one! I've got one!' The fish was beautiful with lovely stripes down its side and a top spiky fin that stood up straight and pricked my hand. Suddenly I was literally hooked on fishing and just knew it was something I wanted to do always. The old fisherman was known as Peg Leg by his mates as he only had one leg. He taught me a lot about fishing. He was a real expert. I forgot about the hops and sat all one day watching him catch bream, some of which weighed up to eight pounds.

David Taylor

Butchers bines

We started at 7.00 a.m. and by the end of the day were wet, muddy and scratched. In the early morning, dew got into the cuts and it stung. Our bines were strung by the butcher's method – a group of four bines tied into a square. The foreman was very strict on how we left the gardens: We couldn't leave leaves or hops lying around on the ground while we were picking, especially at the end of the day. They all had to be picked up and put in the proper places. Once a bine was picked we curled it up like a rope and stacked it neatly, ready for removal later. We got told off if they were left untidy and although they were flexible they were also tough to bend into shape. Another job we had was to collect the wood needed for making a fire or there wouldn't be anything for Mother to cook our dinner on at the end of the day. The faggots were piled twelve feet high so we had to scramble up the stack and throw them down.

Terry Blackman

Hopping back to the early 1900s

My family worked in the hop gardens of Kent before the Second World War. We have hopping photos of my father, uncle and grandparents dating back to 1900s. There is one of a baby in the pram which is me, with my mother, brother and aunt in 1927.

Joan Ellen Wilson (née Barnes)

Picking for Guinness at Bodiam

Guinness was a big business in the Bodiam area of Sussex. They owned many workers' cottages for employees who worked in the gardens all the year round. When the hop gardens started closing down the cottages were sold and I know few people who live there now. Everyone talks about hop picking but forgets the hard work it takes to get them to the picking stage, the drying etc. I was responsible for one acre of hops to train up the strings. There was a lot of work involved and we had to take care when doing the training as if we snapped off the growing tip it meant one less full bine. There was a lot of companionship among the workers, working out in the gardens day after day together. There was no-one else around to talk to and as we only had workers from the local village in the fields we got to know each other very well. When the picking season started in August or September most of Guinness's pickers came down from London on the Hoppers' Special trains so I did not know them. I am eighty-three years of age now but my memories are long and strong. I don't think there is any hand picking today, not round here (Sedlescombe) anyway. It is all done by machine.

Ivy King

The long walk down

My mother had been going all her life, but when she was a young girl she had to walk to Paddock Wood; a thirty mile journey. Her mother and father used to have a bigger cart and she and her brother walked by the cart while the youngest brother sat on the luggage. Mother always reckons that they started out at midnight and were down at Paddock Wood, Kent somewhere about ten o'clock the following day. She often said that only once did they go with a costermonger's barrow and funnily enough it was a bad year and they had to walk home that year so she knew what it was like, walking. The hop farm Mother went to was called White's, which became the Whitbread Hop Farm, Beltring.

Horace Arthur Carr

Problems with those big fivers

We stayed for six weeks on the farm; six weeks of pure heaven for me. I filled my days by picking a few hops, fished a lot, wandered along to the local shop or trekked to the only butchers in the area on errands for Mum. It was a muddy year and I recall very well Sally and I desperately having to pull Tricia's pram along through deep mud going backwards and forwards between the hop field and our hut. We were all happy until it was time to return home. Mum went off to the farmer's house to be paid for all our work. She earned £25 for the six weeks and was paid in five huge white £5 notes. We had never seen so much money before and all studied the notes in awe. We had a job spending them back in Bermondsey as shopkeepers rarely saw fivers and needed a full explanation as to where they had come from before they accepted them.

David Taylor

The brewing process

A simplified version of the process of brewing beer: first an infusion is made of milled barley malt called 'grist' together with brewing liquor. The sweet wort is then separated off from the grains before being boiled up with the hops and sugar. Sugar is optional.

Mark Dobler, former Head Brewer,
Shepherd Neame Brewery

Sad end of the season

The open backed lorry duly arrived. All our possessions were loaded on and we sat there silently as we were borne back to the crowded city, smoke and, for we children, school with all its restrictions. Our one consolation was that we were five weeks late starting the new term. Returning to Bermondsey after the cleanliness and peace of the wonders of Kent was a real shock to the system. The air was so acrid in the city and we missed the damp morning mists. It was like coming home to a miserable world of buildings, traffic and, of course, school, which was definitely not my favourite place to be. The only saving grace was that I could look forward to next year's hopping.

David Taylor

A family of pickers

We were a big family of Hoppers when I was a child. Mother went hop picking for eighty years or more. For over sixty years she picked on the same farm. She was a Londoner but most of us were born in Essex where I live now. She had fifteen children. I was the last one, and I'm eighty-four years old. I still go down to Kent as often as I can and went to the Faversham and Crabtree festivals this year (2003). I wouldn't miss them.

Ann Casson

A fatal illness

My mother became ill. The doctors said that she had a cloud on her lung and needed country air. It was at a time when tuberculosis was very common and the whole family must have been very concerned. The air in Bermondsey was smoky as everyone had coal fires. When it was heavy with dense smog the visibility was down to only a few feet and you couldn't even see the pillar box across the road. It was no place for a person with lung problems. It must have been about August because Mum began talking about going hopping. I was happy because I was due back at school after the summer holidays and I'd rather go anywhere rather than back to school. I hadn't a clue what hopping was but I did know that Dad didn't want her to go. Grannie stepped in and said that she should go if only to get her away from the smog. Dad had a good deal of respect for Grannie and never argued with her. Grandad made us a 4ft x 3ft x 2ft hopping box out of stout timber. He fitted it with pram wheels and a handle so it could be pushed along. He also made a stout wooden bench on which four of us could sit, so we were all ready to go.

David Taylor

Newmarsh Tavern

Mr and Mrs Gordon were the landlord and landlady of Newmarsh Tavern, Belvedere beside the River Thames. Nearby was berthed a yacht and the joint owners were Mr Needham, of North Woolwich and Charles Cooper, my grandfather, who lived at Orient Cottages near The Tavern. As an ex Captain Gunner in the Royal Navy he served on several ships including one of the late Nelson's. Every hopping season the Gordon's hired a charabanc and their men customers went down to the hop fields for a

day's picking. All of us kids were keen to see them off because as the charabanc drove away the men threw out handfuls of coppers (pennies) for us to scramble after and one of the older boys always went as a step boy at the back. Many trips were made with families in the summer. No-one ever locked their doors in those days. Some of the pickers were Mr Ferguson who lived in Johnson's Cottages and was a maintenance engineer at the Borax works, Jim and Henry who were both Corys Lightermen on the barges off Belvedere. Jim Robinson was an ex naval man and lodged at The Tavern. Togo White helped crew the yacht when required. Families enjoyed visiting The Tavern in summer and walking along the riverbank from Erith and Crossness, listening to Peter Cooper play his concertina. Unfortunately The Tavern was bombed in 1940. The locals had all just left for home. The landlords at the time were Mr and Mrs Simmons. They were buried under a pile of rubble when the bomb hit. Fortunately they were rescued and were all right bar a few bruises. My mother, Mrs Cooper, had a lock-up shop and sold sweets and groceries. Every Monday was pickle day. People brought their basins for two penn'orth of mustard pickle or pickled onions for dinner time. We children had to walk one and a quarter miles to school and back for dinner as there weren't any buses.

Ray Cooper

Sally's story

We started hop picking in the summer of 1951. A friend asked Mum if she would like to go picking at Days Farm at Hunton, near Maidstone. Mum liked the idea, so wrote a letter to the farmer to see if she could get a hut and a bin. We were delighted when a reply came to say there was a place available for us with a hut and bin at the end of August. We were delighted and all hell broke out with everyone in the house except Dad. He did not like the idea of Mum going hopping on her own with us. There was me, Sally, aged eleven, my brother David who was eight, little John aged four and Pat who was only fifteen months old. My mum and dad were Daisy and George Taylor.

Sally Nattcutt

Maureen Vinall's mum with Daisy, Peggy and Len Vinall (Maureen's husband-to-be) and Ben, her father, at Chambers Farm enjoying a well-deserved tea break.

Hopping at Bodiam

Some days we kids went fishing, even in the moat surrounding Bodiam Castle opposite the railway station. The hops were collected twice daily, our tally of bushels picked was noted by the book keeper and entered in each picker's book so they knew how much pay was owed. The hops in their pokes were transported to the oast house by horse and cart. This was pulled by two lovely grey Shire horses; one was Prince; I can't remember the other's name. During the evenings Hoppers sat round the fires singing the old songs and joking. During the Saturday evenings some adults walked over to the Castle pub at Bodiam. It is still there. Other villagers from nearby went home for the weekends. We younger ones had a great time; it was the time of our lives. It was really hard work for our parents; a busman's holiday in fact.

Alfred H. Robinson

Our first hopping holiday

The day arrived when we were to go hopping. We pushed the hopping box, full of clothes, pots and pans to Jamaica Road together with the bench and a huge Navy kitbag containing blankets for our bedding. There was Mum, Sally who was ten years old, me aged seven, John who was three and Tricia, who was only eighteen months old sitting in a huge old-fashioned pram, and the cat. It was about 5.00 a.m. at the beginning of September and there we were, waiting for a lorry to arrive to take us down hopping. An open-backed lorry duly arrived loaded with smiling people, prams, dogs, cats and a mountain of luggage. Somehow all our luggage was loaded on with us all perched precariously on top of it and we started off into the wilds of Kent with the lorry grinding its way up and down steep country roads. Eventually we turned off the road and splashed along a muddy

Maureen Vinall's mum's friend, father (Ben), and other of mum's friends; Peggy and Ben Vinall, Maureen's future husband, on Chambers Farm.

lane into a huge field thronged with people playing about and laughing happily. This indeed was a happy place and dozens of children were running around, while women shook loose bales of straw outside the rows of tin huts, built in lines on the field. We saw fires glowing with huge steaming pots hanging above them. There were piles of faggots outside each hut; these were bundles of tree prunings. As well, there were two bales of straw for each hut. I was still perched on the lorry but was already beginning to feel that I liked hopping.

David Taylor

Getting our own back

We used to go down hopping in a lorry and on the way we passed lots of signs outside pubs saying 'No hop pickers' which really annoyed us. In the last year we went down by charabanc and deliberately stopped at all those places that had barred us when

we were on the lorry. We were pleased because as we were all posh in a charabanc, they served us instead of turning us away.

Ivy Dixon (née Smith)

Down in the gardens

Mother, myself and Gran had two bins to fill. When Gran picked she put everything in; leaves, bits of bine, the lot. Of course it was we boys who got blamed for it when the measurer came round. My brother and I picked straight into the sacks and these were emptied into the bin before the measurer arrived. He would look at all the leaves and say 'You boys give me real work to do!' Mum was a wonderfully fast picker and would often pass us working on one row as she picked on another by herself. We got really black hands from the hop juice but that didn't worry us as children.

Terry Blackman

Hart Green Farm, 1920s. Three men with hop dogs used for grubbing out the 25ft poles when they needed replacing. (Courtesy of Mrs. D. Isaacs)

Van arriving at Harts Green Farm from Ebdens Hill with hop pickers from Hastings in 1920. (Courtesy of Mrs. D. Isaacs)

Aside from hopping

Even though the mornings were freezing and the hop bines were soaking wet we managed all right and still had a wonderful time. David hated picking but would stay on helping Mum until lunchtime and spent most of the afternoons fishing down at the river. He nearly always met someone else who was keen and stayed a fisherman all his life.

We came back from hopping all happy and brown and could not wait for the following year. Mum had a few pounds in her pocket to spend, too.

Sally Nattcutt

A village with three pubs

There were three public houses in Horsemonden in the old days and my father Alan's pub The Town House was the most popular with

85

The Town House and King's Arms Hotel at Horsmonden in 1935. Mrs. Palmer's family owned the popular Town House.

Hoppers. The other two pubs in the village were The Gun and the King's Arms. The latter is now converted into a private house. There isn't room for three pubs in a small village these days although they still hold the annual Gypsies Fair on The Green. A picture postcard of The Town House was sent to Mrs H. Tile at 'Sunniside', St Georges Road, Bexhill-on-Sea by her Auntie Lu and Cousin Kitty. It reads 'Dear Gladys, Auntie Lu and I came here on Friday. We come to you next Friday so please book our room for a fortnight. Hop picking begins here tomorrow, The Green looks very busy. David is getting excited looking forward to seeing you all. With love, Auntie Lu and Kitty.' It was posted from Tonbridge in September 1935.

D. Palmer

A new world

Mum adored the countryside and she was very happy down there. She was by nature a happy person, never one to moan and was a most understanding, kind and good listener if anyone had a problem. She was always laughing and helping others. Once we settled down in our little tin hut it was like being in a new world, although for Mum it must all have been very hard work with four small children to look after as well as pick the hops and do the cooking. I

was excited by this newly found freedom and asked Mum if I could go exploring. Mum gave permission but warned me not to go near the Medway. I didn't know what a Medway was and was too keen on the idea of exploring to stop and ask. I wandered across the field in amongst all the huts. The grass was long and as I walked dozens of horseflies flew up, disturbed by my feet. I saw lines of children wandering the fields away in the distance and went across to where they were. When I got near I realised they were walking along the banks of a beautiful river. The water was clear and I could see shoals of fish just below the surface. There were large areas of water lilies, marsh plants, willow trees and reed beds. For me, freshly arrived from Bermondsey, it was paradise. I wandered timelessly for a while before returning to Mum and our old tin hut.

David Taylor

Songs around the camp fire

Dad used to pop down on a Saturday with Mum's housekeeping but although he stayed the night we knew he did not like it. Each Saturday evening we all sat around the camp fire and someone would come down with an accordion and play all the old songs for us to sing. We stuck potatoes on the end of sticks and cooked them in the embers of the fire. It was grand. As the years went on I started to work but still came down hopping from Friday night to Sunday. By then all the local boys would come to the common to suss out the 'talent' and we always had lads sitting round our fire. Mum used to make them sausage sandwiches. I think that was the main reason they stayed.

Sally Nattcutt

Thrown in the hop bin

A lady in her late fifties came to visit Bough Beech visitors' centre one day and told us her hop picking reminiscences. 'When the picking was all finished the farmer threw me in the last bin of hops if I was naughty' she said. I told this to the elderly farmer who had run the hop farm where they had picked and he went away chuckling, so probably remembered when it happened.

Joan Medill

Barrel taps. These wooden taps were made on a foot-driven lathe.

A bung is a shive

I know some people call it a bung and say 'Bung it in the hole' but its real name is a shive and they're the wooden stopper that goes in the hole at the top of the barrel to control the air flow. I made shives for twenty-seven years for C. Olley's business. We made them for Charringtons, Tate & Lyle and other big firms. They'd tell us what size and shape they wanted then we'd use a lathe and make them out of cork, hazel, oak, pine or beech wood going by what was needed. We often used off-cuts as these were cheaper than buying new lengths of wood. We could make twenty-five gross in a day; that's 3,600 shives a day, or 18,000 in a week.

We cut the shives from the top to get a small hole, then from the other end to get a bigger hole underneath but we didn't go right through to the other side – just so the bottom of the small hole was drilled level with the top of the bigger (lower) hole. The shives were cut 3/4' thick and we drilled them down two-thirds on an automatic machine which also made a ring cut round the outside. The sides of the shive were tapered so they would fit snugly into the barrel hole then they were all put into a big tub which was tumbled until they were smooth and shiny with no rough parts. The shives were tapped into the holes on the tops of barrels then, after they were filled with beer, wine, treacle or whatever the brewer or manufacturer produced, they were sent off to the retailers.

George Maddock and Elsie

Queueing – a British way of life

Junction Road, do you know that? It was all Guinness's here of course. There were several camps. Coming from Cripps Corner down on the Junction Road to Hawkhurst, as you come down right in the hollow there was Craneham Camp on the right-hand side. You went over the little single track railway and there was Park Farm and then there was Kell Farm on the road that actually comes out here by Ockham, then we used to walk through from there to Bodiam on a Sunday or go up to the Junction pub for a drink and a bag of crisps and a lemonade, that sort of thing. And that was sixty-one years ago and the only fault was when there were dog fights

Pickers at Harts Green Farm. 1920s. (Courtesy of Mrs. D. Isaacs)

in the air over the hop fields when the war was on. The butcher and grocer from Hawkhurst came down and you'd queue up for hours waiting for the food. But because we were classified as agricultural workers – essential work – you got extra rations, so instead of an ounce of cheese which was the usual ration per person during the war, we got three-quarters of a pound, but it was usually ever so rancid and horribly strong. I've written about our family for the grandchildren and made it into a book and a lot of it is about how I was a child in the war with the hop picking. We actually live in an oast now; we don't live in the oast itself, we live in the farm but the oast has not been converted, it's as it was. It's still got the slatted floor which is nearly all complete. We've not got the press. That's in Linfield near Bexhill.

Anne and Brian Feist

'God's good earth'

Over the years Mum kept hop picking but only with Pat and John as my brother Dave and I were working full time. She went to Headcorn, then to Paddock Wood and kept picking hops for as long as she had a hut to go to. When the hand picking stopped we used to take Mum down to Days Farm at least once a year. She loved it there. She called it 'God's good earth'. It brought back so many memories for her. We really roughed it with the weather and the awful mud and seemed

to spend most of our time in Wellington boots but I would not have missed it for the world.

Sally Nattcutt

How to dress a large family using hops!

My mother-in-law had thirteen children, half of whom were girls. They lived in Romney Marsh. They went to Paddock Wood to pick. At the end of the week when they had finished, mother-in-law took the family in to Rye to buy a bolt of cloth with the money they'd earned, then used it to make all the girls new dresses.

Irene Feist

Small pleasures

Mum sometimes picked at Marden as well as Bodiam, but we children did all our picking at the Guinness fields. The toilets were right down the bottom of a long field. All our cooking was done outside on an open fire whether it was meat or vegetables. We enjoyed scrumping as boys; apples, plums, whatever was going. We usually went after dinner as there was nothing else for us children to go out for in the evenings. Mum sometimes went down to the local pub with the others and if she did she brought us back some arrowroot biscuits which were a real treat.

Terry Blackman

Ladies up the pole

We were on a Sunday school trip when the subject of hop picking came up and a posh lady looked at us and said 'Poor things! I do wonder how some of the dears get up those tall poles to pick the hops?' which told us she had never seen hop pickers working. We went home laughing at the silly idea of all our mums trying to climb hop poles to get at the hops.

Pat Walkling

Signs of the times

Many years after the hop picking stopped, when I had two children of my own and my son was eight years old and my daughter was five we took them to Days Farm for the day for a picnic. The old tin hopping huts had been pulled down but our brick hut was still there. Our son just could not believe that we could have lived in a place like that but then he didn't know the happy times we had and, given the opportunity to find out, I am sure he would have loved it. My late brother, David Taylor, was awarded an MBE for his road safety work, giving talks to children in schools. He was renowned for riding round the Isle of Man TT race circuit on one wheel of his motorbike and was nick-named The Wheelie King.

Sally Nattcutt

Mostly, memories are all that's left of hopping

Now I am a grown man in my sixties with children and grandchildren of my own, I feel it is a great shame – indeed a tragedy – that the machine has taken over the picking of hops, denying my children and generations of children to come one of the most wonderful experiences of my and their lifetimes. We picked at several farms, including Marshall's Farm at Lamberhurst, Nightingale Farm at Southborough as well as one-day Sunday picking on quite a few farms where we worked for pickers, finishing off their nearly completed fields. Dundle Farm at Kipping's Cross was the only place where we stayed in the hopper's huts. If I was given just one wish – to be able to do just one thing in all of this wonderful world – it would be without doubt the chance of spending a month in fantastic September weather, picking hops around a hop bin with my darling Mum and Dad (Ethel and George Connor), my brother Brian, my four sisters, Gaye, Jill, Jackie and Susan and listen to the sound of Hoppers and hop picking with all the sights and sounds I remember so well. It is only a simple wish which, sadly, can never come true.

Patrick Connor

A ditch used as an air-raid shelter

There were plenty of air raids around the hop fields during the war and our 'air-raid shelter' was a ditch at the side of the lane. If the air raid sirens sounded during our time in the hop garden it was into the nearest ditch or hedge to get out of sight as enemy fighter aircraft sometimes shot at us as they flew overhead. One amusing recollection was of our ARP (Air Raid Precaution) warden who was, unfortunately, hard of hearing, so usually she was the last person among us to hear the alarm.

Alfred H. Robinson

11 When Two Hoppers Reminisce

You're never too young to go hopping. Watched by father Mauro, Dominic tries on grandma's hopping hat.

Ex-Hoppers always have plenty of tales to tell; you can't keep a good Hopper down. During the Kent and East Sussex Railway Hop Festival, September 2003, hundreds of ex-Hoppers came to celebrate the hopping season around the railway station and to tell me their reminiscences. Get two Hoppers together and the memories fly swiftly. Two men had originally come to speak to me and started telling me their individual tales but, as they had hopped at the same farm, eventually ended by talking to each other. They were still there sharing memories as we sat round the camp fire enjoying our evening's hot supper together. There was no need for me in this conversation so I switched on the tape recorder and here is a record of their recollections:

−'When we came down from London we were told we had to be at the main line station in time to get the train at five o'clock in the morning because all the hopping boxes had to be loaded on the train.'

−'I remember that. And when we were down picking we were actually out in the fields by about a quarter to seven'

−'That's right. I have got a lot of good memories, but I've got a lot of hard memories too.'

−'Yes they were hard. I've always said they were tough times.'

−'Do you remember when the Bishop of Stepney used to come down to the hop fields and he sometimes used to bring students down with him?.'

−'Yes, one year they were American students.'

−'The first time I ever heard of *South Pacific* was when this American fellow done it when they did a show for us down in the Hopfield.'

−'I remember it well.'

−'Do you remember the wet fish that used to come round?'

−'That's right. It wasn't cooked and it was kept cold with ice.'

−'The cod or haddock we could buy… it used to be lovely, and the old Hotspur cake we used to buy covered in pink cream.'

−'Last year I went down that road to the farm and Crownham woods.'

−'I know where you mean and you know that apple tree, where you see the apple orchard?'

−'Yes I know.'

−'Well if you look up there you can see the old farmhouse. Yes, well I was looking at the entrance, because you had an entrance into Crownham Woods and opposite there was another entrance where the shop used to be.'

−'That's right, and I found the old oast houses where they used to put the hops. They were a fair old way away.'

−'And do you remember old Mr Jarvis? He used

to come round on his horse at seven o'clock in the morning to make sure everyone was out. And me and my nephews and cousins, mostly cousins, well we mostly had dogs so about nine o'clock I used to say to my mum "I've got to go to the toilet" and we'd go round and collect the others and the dogs then we'd go off for the day! There was a farmer up near Staplecross and he had three sons and two of them had to go off to war in the army and one had to stay on the farm and we used to go and help him. His wife used to make these marvellous meat and potato pies. I can still remember the taste. She made us cold tea, because that used to quench your thirst.'

–'Pop bottles, do you remember them?'

–'The kind that you pushed in?'

–'No, no, you had to swivel the top.'

–'The old pub that used to sell them is still there, isn't it? We used our subs for a night out.'

–'Yes. Well as kids, from Crownham Woods we used to have to walk up to Staplecross one way or to the Junction the other way. Why is it called The Junction do you know?'

–'No, I don't know. It wasn't anything to do with the railway because that junction is over the other way.'

–'Yes, the old umbrella field's there still isn't it? It's got all apples in it now.'

–'Yes and do you remember at Park Farm when they had that fire?'

–'Yes that was bad. We used to get the old lorries there in them days to put them (fires) out? 'Cos they were so far apart weren't they?'

–'I remember that. One was called Oxford and the other was called Cambridge. It all comes back now.'

–'This is a pilgrimage I have to make every year, back to the hop gardens.'

–'Well, my wife's the same. She loves to come down here and remember the old days.'

–'You used to be able to walk right through here and the old houses that were down at the bottom are still there.'

–'Are they? I know there used to be a pathway all the way through and as you got down to the pond…'

–'That's right, the pond's still there.'

–'…there's a farm there, and you might think I'm being funny but I'm not really, that farm there was owned by a Mr Stevens. It was open for children to go and have a look at the animals…Quarry Farm…well I took my granddaughter there and as I got to the farm and stopped and when I got out of the car I said to my granddaughter "I've been here before. I have, I've been here" and I stopped the farmer and asked him and he said "Yes, this is Crownham Woods. If you'd like to down here and along the path, look up the top there and that's where the huts were." I remembered it all so well.'

–'Well I was speaking to a fellow over at the Castle and he said if you go into there you can

One of the pleasures of being in the countryside, for town folk, is seeing the animals. Here a gaggle of geese make their way back from a stream.

Visitors (at rear) from London attending hop picking family at Harts Green. (Courtesy of Mrs. D. Isaacs)

still see the wooden posts in the ground where the huts used to be standing. They're still there. But a lot of it now is for horses, for steeplechasers, they run round over the back there because it's got the jumps and everything.'

−'We used to walk along the railway to Robertsbridge and then along this lane, the other way to go over to Bodiam.'

−'Sometimes we used what was called a jimmy-john with two handles you had to pump up and down to go along the rails.'

−'I remember. It was like in the old *Carry On* and *St Trinian's* films.'

−'That's right. We went to that Paddock Wood Festival. We were there a couple of weeks ago but it was nothing like where we went. They were on there about Carnival Queens and all that and I was trying to tell them we'd not got time for anything like that. We were too busy picking.'

−'We went on strike; all the area. Do you remember that?'

−'Yes, was it three bushels for sixpence or something we were getting?'

−'Something like that. It's unbelievable. People just don't realise, do they? They wouldn't have that! Especially my old Mum. My old granddad was bad enough.'

−'They say that some years hopping was bad but other years it was terrible. If they were small that was it; it would take you all day, practically, just

to get a bushel.'

−'And you'd watch the old bin bloke and made sure he didn't stuff the hops down too tight.'

−'It all depended on what type of measurer you had. If you got a good bloke then he'd flick a few out for you.'

−'It depended what kind of hops you were picking, too. If they were big cones you were all right, but then if there were too many leaves in it …we came down here for eight weeks. Yes, eight weeks. It was the best holiday I ever had.'

−'Mind you I used to get into trouble when I went back to school. They laughed at me when I told them it was the only holiday my Mum and Dad could afford, it was true, mind, but I'd say "While you're at school I'm still out there having the time of my life".'

−'But do you remember what it was like pulling those bines…?'

−'When it was wet through…'

−'The first thing in the morning the dew went all down your neck.'

−'Some of us wore sacks round our necks to stop it going down.'

−'Well I tell you my bine was brilliant again this year, and the whole of my shed was covered. I think the weather did it, and the aroma's so strong…'

−'Do you know we even used to come hopping in the war…'

Freddie Ganny and friend

12 Growing Your Own Hops

The call of the bine never ends. 'Come back to Sorrento' was a popular song of the 1950s but it seems Sorrento cannot compete with an Englishman's Hopfield once the 'bug' has bitten. 'You can keep your Capri, Benidorm and Las Palmas. As far as I'm concerned, give me a holiday in a good old Sussex hop garden with all my pals around me, singing those old Music Hall songs any day of the week' I was told recently by a visitor to the Kent and East Sussex Railway Hop Festival. 'If it started up again tomorrow I'd be back among the bines, picking as if my life depended on it' another ex-Hopper said.

When making beer only female cones are used in the process. This is because, unlike male flowers, which are pollen producers, each female petal is ribbed with tiny veins a mere 0.5 mm wide, which hold the oils essential to beer making and responsible for beer's bitter taste. It facilitates in the preservation of malted barley. With this in mind, it is easy to understand why a hop garden usually consists entirely of female plants. Like cattle, where only one bull is needed to fertilize a whole herd of cows, so one male hop plant is all that is needed to fertilize many female hop plants.

Mainly out of nostalgia, and only occasionally because they want to make their own beer, Hoppers frequently ask how they may obtain and grow their own hop plant. I hope the following information will be useful and help you to establish your own flourishing, bountiful bine.

'How do I get a hop plant to start with?' you ask. The simplest way to obtain the hop crown or plant is to purchase one from a hop garden, hop festival or garden centre in August or September. Some places where hop crowns can be bought are: The Hop Farm Country Park in Paddock Wood, formerly Whitbread's Hop Farm; Great Knelle Farm, Beckley, East Sussex (01797 260321/250); Essentially Hops, Parsonage Farm, Bekesbourne, Kent, CT4 5ER (www.essentiallyhops.co.uk) and The Kent Museum for Rural Life at Cobham. Most working hop farms usually have hop crowns available for sale. These vary in price according to type but will currently cost between £7 and £12 each. Expect to pay more for a specialist variety. Individual hop farmers may be willing to let you have one of the more striking kinds. Fuggles are known for their large, attractive cones but if your garden is small it may be best to look for a dwarf variety to ensure it won't be taken over by a twenty-five or thirty-foot bine anxious to find and overwhelm something tall to cling to such as your clothes post or garden shed.

There are several traditional ways of establishing a bine but the most assured method is to buy the rhizome or crown of a year-old plant from a reputable seller who knows what he/she is talking about when you mention 'hops'. Another method explained by an ex-Hopper visiting the Kent and East Sussex Railway Hop Festival, is to tear off a piece of hop plant making sure there is a heel from the stem, dip this in hormone powder, fill a plastic shopping bag with potting compost, firm the hop heel into the compost, water well (but don't drown it!) then tie up the top of the bag and leave for a few (unspecified) weeks to establish. I am assured that after this time the cutting will have developed roots and as soon as these are sufficiently strong for the plant to maintain its own growth unaided it can be transplanted into a very large plant pot or directly into the garden and allowed to mature... don't forget to prepare the ground before planting it out. The crown must not be planted directly into fresh manure or compost which will burn the roots. It is best to prepare the ground a month in advance, digging in a generous amount of bone meal, horse or chicken manure or home-made garden compost well mixed with soil and leaving a 30cm/12 inch deep hole ready for the hop plant. Some keen growers have been known to establish a plant by growing it in a large beer barrel on the patio but this requires close attention to the root development as otherwise it will eventually burst the barrel.

It must be remembered that, when growing naturally, hops establish rooting systems of up to five or six feet deep after the first couple of years, so it will need to be planted in a suitable part of the garden unless you intend to keep lightly trimming the roots to stunt its growth. As spring brings the warmer weather, hop tendrils begin to appear and by July bines will be half way up their supports. Development during the first year will be relatively slow but, once the root stock is established, progress will be vigorous. To ensure the success of your plant's growth here are some essential rules you should follow: rhizomes should be planted horizontally, not upright. During the growing season (spring to summer) the plant needs watering daily (particularly during its first year), regular feeding and dusting with 'Nimrod' or similar blight control. If establishing more than one hop crown, plant them at least three feet apart. Be careful not to break delicate tendril tips as they will stop growing. Hop bines are heavy when full grown so need firm support; plant near a tall fence, wall or pole or fix strong string netting to an overhead wire to which tendrils can cling as they get taller. An ideal support would be a garden arch or gazebo. Shoots grow up to 15cm per day in a warm summer so need to be regularly twirled up the support until they reach full height. Rough twine is easier for the plant to climb than nylon line as the tendrils find difficulty in grasping the smooth surface of nylon

or plastic. Hops prefer a sunny, well drained position but are not too choosy about the soil type (mine are growing enthusiastically in a heavy clay area but most Kent and East Sussex hop gardens are chalk-based.) Established plants develop a healthy crop of a dozen or more tendrils during spring but these need to be reduced to four or five and no more than eight of the healthiest shoots or growth will be over-vigorous with 'pipey' (weak) bines. As plants develop, hoe weeds regularly from around the hill. Mulch around the base with organic compost or manure but keep it away from the roots and bine itself. To keep bines free of pests, dust regularly with a suitable insecticide of a kind not absorbed by the plant, such as 'Nimrod', available from garden centres. Keep the bottom 15-20cm of stems free of leaves as this helps the plant to stay healthy. Hop cones are ripe once there is a sign of the first few beginning to turn brown. Bines to be used for decoration need picking straight away to stop the petals dropping. Hops are best harvested in dry weather and need careful drying for use in brewing. Do not dry them in hot, direct sunlight or they will burn and lose both flavour and aroma. Try using your hops for hop pillows if you want a good night's sleep. They can be mixed with lavender. As long as the cones are spread out flat to allow for even ventilation, drying can be done by one of several methods: on a low heat in the microwave; in an oven on the lowest possible temperature; on a flat clothes-drying screen in the open air or by using a food dehydrator if you have one. Ensure hops are thoroughly dried before storage or they will rot. The petals should feel papery.

Hop plants can last up to forty years if well cared for. Bines should be pruned to a few inches above ground level in autumn as this encourages them to rejuvenate for next season. The cones or flowers are decorative and may be dried for indoor ornamentation. If dried properly and undisturbed they will last until next year's fresh growth is ready to replace them.

Glossary

Ale: alcoholic infusion made of fermented malt with a bittering agent such as hops. Henry VIII disliked the taste of hops and decreed his ale should be brewed without hop flavouring. Nowadays ale is usually made with the addition of hops.

Amylase: a type of carbohydrate, being dextrin, starch, insulin, glycogen, cellulose, tunicin and gum, all with the composition of $C_6H_{10}O_5$.

Aroma Hops: Also called flavouring hops. These are special hops which impart a particular, defined flavour to each brand of beer.

Barrel: wooden cask, the sides of which are formed from wooden staves curved by steaming and bending, then shaved so that both ends taper slightly and when fastened together by metal hoops, bulge slightly round the middle giving it a strong, damage resistant shape. Barrel makers are known as coopers. By tradition, an apprentice was required to make a barrel of high standard to prove he was worthy of becoming a cooper. He was then put inside his own barrel and rolled down a hill. If the barrel (and the apprentice!) survived the journey the apprentice passed his articles.

Beer: generic term for any fermented liquor such as beer, ale, porter, small (weak) beer, etc. It is likely that the brewing of beer was first begun in this country by monks of foreign orders bringing hop plants with them to grow in monastery gardens when settling in Britain.

Bine: a hop vine. Bines 'follow the sun'; that is they grow upwards in a clockwise direction, whereas most other climbers climb anti-clockwise. Bine leaves are similar to those of the grape vine.

Bittering hops: used for the bulk of beer

Formerly used to haul drays of beer kegs, Whitbread's beautiful Shire horses now enjoy a more leisurely life at the Hop Farm Country Park in Paddock Wood.

brewing before other ingredients are added.

Bright beer: clear and uncloudy.

Cask: a barrel; from the French *casque*. Used as a container for beer.

Cattle cake: made from spent hops after brewing.

Dray: heavy, horse drawn cart pulled by one or two dray horses. These can still be seen in parades and at county shows and The Hop Farm Country Park in Paddock Wood retains their famous 'grey' Shire horses which are on public show throughout most of the year. During the summer visitors can ride on a horse-pulled dray around the hop farm.

Firkin: medieval Dutch word for a small cask, holding a quarter of a barrel, for liquids and fish. Formerly eight gallons; now nine gallons.

Garden (Hop): also hop field, hop yard. Where hops are grown.

Hill: originally hops were planted into mounds of earth two or three feet high called hills. Later practice meant that earth was not built up and hops were planted straight into the ground with a small mound of earth encircling it but the name 'hill' continued in use.

Hops: flowers or cones of a perennial hop bine.

Hop dog: implement combining a straight and a curved blade fixed on a pole; used to cut down tough stems of hop bines.

Hop garden: fields of hops belonging to a particular farm.

Hop infestations: The hop, while being a hardy plant, is subject to destructive attacks from various parasites and fungi such as hop fleas or beetles; forms of aphids such as hop-fly, frog or froth fly; mildew and other blights. Early spraying with fungicide or nicotine can prevent or minimise the problem but once a garden has blight it usually has to be totally destroyed and everything and everyone associated with the garden must be disinfected to prevent the disease from spreading.

Hopper: hop picker; a vat for infusing hops before adding to the wort.

Keg: small barrel usually used as a container for lager and containing less than ten gallons.

Hopsacking: rough material woven from jute and/or hemp for making pockets or pokes. Also, in medieval times when social status dictated the kind of fabric from which a person's clothing could be made (silk and linen being for the elevated classes,) hopsacking was considered suitable for serfs, villains or peasants.

Kilderkin: capacity measure. A small cask holding between sixteen and eighteen gallons of liquid.

Liquor: brewer's term for the pure water used in the process of brewing.

Maltings: also known as Ale Grains; residue left after completion of the brewing process. Consists of spent hops, malt and yeast. Popular as a pick-me-up feed with both horses and cattle but, due to its potency and (much as alcohol affects human beings) too much can intoxicate! Supplies in Australia are more difficult to obtain than in UK as sales tend to be limited to racing establishments.

Mash: crushed malt mixed with hot water to form wort.

Oast: building for processing hops. Consists of a roundel where hops are roasted over a furnace, drying floor, ram for packing hops tightly into pockets and storage for the filled pockets waiting to be sold.

Poke: sack used to convey hops from the hop field to the Oast house for roasting. Smaller than a pocket, it holds ten bushels.

Pocket: diminutive of poke. A hop-sacking bag some 180cm long and 45cm wide used for tightly packing and storing dried hops to be sent to the buyers or hop factors. Holds 150 bushels.

Roundel: The round (or square) tower of an oast.

Sack: large bag made from coarse cloth of hemp or flax. Nowadays, any sized bag made from sacking.

Shive: correct name for a barrel bung.

Sparge: Sprinkle wort with liquor during the brewing process.

Sparl: small wooden wedge used to open the shive in a barrel to let air in, allowing the contents to flow without hindrance.

Stout: a brew made from black malt which gives it its distinctive flavour and colour.

Tun: early eigtheenth-century English word. Generally, a large cask or barrel, particular to brewing; a fermenting or mashing vat. Also a specific liquid measure: In mediaeval times this was 252 old wine gallons, two pipes, or four hogsheads. Sometimes seen as part of a public house name: The Three Tuns etc.

Wort: a brew or infusion of malted barley which, when added to hops, causes fermentation.

If you are interested in purchasing other books published by Tempus, or in case you have difficulty finding any Tempus books in your local bookshop, you can also place orders directly through our website

www.tempus-publishing.com

or from

BOOKPOST, Freepost, PO Box 29, Douglas, Isle of Man IM99 1BQ
Tel 01624 836000   email bookshop@enterprise.net